Also by Peter Walsh

It's All Too Much
An Easy Plan for Living a Richer Life with Less

Does This Clutter Make My Butt Look Fat?
An Easy Plan for Losing Weight and Living More

Enough Already!
Clearing Mental Clutter to Become the Best You

How To Organize (Just About) Everything
More Than 500 Step-by-Step Instructions
for Everything from Organizing Your Closets
to Planning a Wedding to Creating
a Flawless Filing System

The Tools You Need
To Conquer Clutter
and Create the Life
You Want

It's All Too Much
Workbook

PETER WALSH

FREE PRESS
New York   London   Toronto   Sydney

Free Press
A Division of Simon & Schuster, Inc.
1230 Avenue of the Americas
New York, NY 10020

First Free Press trade paperback edition April 2009

FREE PRESS and colophon are trademarks
of Simon & Schuster, Inc.

For information about special discounts for bulk purchases,
please contact Simon & Schuster Special Sales at
1-866-506-1949 or business@simonandschuster.com.

The Simon & Schuster Speakers Bureau can bring authors to your live event.
For more information or to book an event contact the Simon & Schuster Speakers
Bureau at 1-866-248-3049 or visit our website at simonspeakers.com.

Designed by Katy Riegel

Manufactured in the United States of America

10 9 8 7 6 5 4 3 2 1

Library of Congress Cataloging-in-Publication Data

Walsh, Peter
    It's all too much workbook : the tools you need to conquer clutter and create the life
you want / by Peter Walsh. —1st American paperback ed.
        p.   cm.
    Companion to the author's It's all too much : an easy plan for living a richer life with
less stuff.
    1. Storage in the home.   2. Orderliness.   3. House cleaning.   I. Walsh, Peter, 1956–
It's all too much.   II. Title.
    TX309.W342   2009
    648'.8—dc22
                                                                    2009009744

ISBN-13: 978-1-4391-4956-0
ISBN-10:   1-4391-4956-9

To all those who—
after looking at their stuff
and screaming "It's all too much"—
have embraced the idea that less is more and,
in decluttering and getting organized,
have created amazing new lives.
Thank you.

Contents

PART I—MY BEAUTIFUL HOUSE   1

1. Conquering Clutter   3

2. Your Home   15

3. Putting Clutter in Its Place   37

4. The Master Bedroom   67

5. Kids' Rooms   101

6. Family and Living Rooms   127

7. Home Office   153

8. Kitchen   173

9. Dining Room   195

10. Bathroom   205

11. Garage, Basement, and Other Storerooms   215

12. Sanctuary   229

x

Contents

PART II—KEEPING IT CLUTTER-FREE   233

13. Maintenance   235

14. Cleanup Checkup   247

15. New Rituals   253

16. Control the Inflow   271

Appendix   277

Resources   281

Clutter stops us from living in the present.

Clutter makes us forget what is really important.

Clutter robs us of real value.

Clutter steals our space.

Clutter monopolizes our time.

Clutter takes over.

Clutter jeopardizes our relationships.

Other people's clutter robs us of opportunities that should be ours.

Clutter denies us peace of mind.

Clutter erodes our spiritual selves.

At the end of the day, clutter makes us forget what's really important.

Part I
My Beautiful House

Conquering Clutter

WE TOOK A JOURNEY TOGETHER in *It's All Too Much* where I introduced you to a systematic program that I developed from my years as a clutter expert, going into hundreds of homes and seeing firsthand the challenges that we all face in living the fast paced, hectic lives that seem to have become the norm for so many. With this workbook I will give you the tools you need to maintain a clutter-free life and to be sure that you will change your relationship with stuff for the long haul—daily, weekly, monthly, and for the rest of your life.

This workbook should be your companion as you work to declutter your personal spaces and your life. It will become the place that you write down your vision for the home you want to live in as a reflection of your values, goals, and dreams. It will help you track your progress and be a place where you can take an inventory of what you are holding on to (perhaps for the wrong reasons); what you are surrounding yourself with on a daily basis; and what you can let go of to make room for the life you want.

I'm sure you have made great progress by doing the work I outlined for you in *It's All Too Much* and you should be proud of what you have accomplished. Please keep in mind that sometimes a first round of decluttering isn't enough. A few months later you'll look at the same stuff you thought you couldn't throw out and realize that you haven't touched it since your last cleanup. It takes a while to get used to the idea that if you don't use it, if it's not part of your life, if it doesn't serve your goals, then it is just a waste of space.

In this workbook we are going to put a laser-like focus on where your problem areas may be lurking. You know what I mean—the stack of shoe boxes in the back of the closet, the storage containers in the basement stuffed with things you've carried with you since college, the expensive sweater you'll wear when it fits again—someday. We're going to pull all of these things out into the light of day and, like the space and energy vampires they are, they will be vanquished. Sometimes we can look without really seeing what's there. My hope for this workbook is that you will use it to create the habits (daily, weekly, monthly) that will help keep you clutter free for life.

Remember, your home is where you live, breathe, rest, love, eat, and create and there should be ample space and room to serve those needs.

In *It's All Too Much* we looked at how clutter gets in the way of living the lives we're meant to live. Because you have this workbook in your hands, I know you are ready to dig deeper (literally) and get rid of the stuff that is getting in your way. Some of the work in *It's All Too Much* may have gone smoothly for you; other parts were probably a little more challenging. Give yourself a pat on the back for what you have achieved by your work so far. I know you are ready now to take a closer look at what is around you and see the areas that really need your attention.

CLUTTER QUESTIONS

You are not going to be graded on your answers to the following questions. They are designed to get you thinking about the current state of your home and plant the seeds for how you would like to see it change:

Do you feel comfortable having people visit your home?

_____

Do you need to clear off the kitchen counter to prepare a meal?

_____

Are the small appliances that you rarely, if ever, use on the counter or in a cupboard?

_____

Could you have a party without cleaning up first?

_____

Do you have a stash of plastic bags that seems to grow daily?

_____

Do your clothes fit in your closet?

_____

Do all of your clothes fit you?

_____

Do you regularly misplace your car keys or checkbook?

_____

Can you work at your desk?

_____

Where are this month's bills?

_____

Are last month's bills paid and the relevant paperwork filed away?

_____

If you had to do your taxes right now, could you find the relevant papers?

_____

When was the last time you used your dining room table for dining?

_____

Do you have to remove laundry, toys, and/or children to get to your bed?

_____

How many magazines do you have in the house? Where are they?

_____

How many catalogs do you have in the house? Where are they?

_____

Where is the remote control for the TV, DVD, CD player, game console?

_____

Are books, DVDs, CDs, video games threatening to take over your family room?

_____

Is there laundry waiting to be put away?

_____

Is there a box (or two) somewhere that you never unpacked from your last move?

_____

Did you unpack all of your wedding gifts? Are you using them?

_____

Do you have any of your belongings in storage?

_____

When was the last time you went to the storage facility? Do you even remember what you are storing?

_____

Are you using the top of the television as a shelf?

_____

Is your floor clear of papers, toys, magazines, newspapers, shoes, clothes?

_____

On any given day, what is the state of the bedrooms in your house?

_____

How about your dining room and your kitchen? _____

_____

What does your garage look like? Can you use it to park your car?

_____

In the following pages you will be making lists, writing down thoughts, feelings, and ideas, cataloging your possessions, and figuring out what's truly important and what holds meaning for your life. But the answers to the questions above will help you figure out which areas of your home should be the first ones you work on clearing out.

If you know anything about me you know that I believe the problem behind clutter isn't the stuff itself but how we think about our stuff and what we do, or don't do, about it that causes problems. Everyone has an excuse for how their home got into its present state: from not enough space to not enough time to not enough help. I've heard them all and have found that most people choose to mislabel their excuses as *reasons*. The *reason* I can't clean up is _____. You call it a reason, I see an excuse. Words can be powerful. What we say to ourselves repeatedly we come to believe. However, if we speak back to the excuse, we can overcome it. The exercise below should be done for every room and every object that is cluttering your home and life.

KNOCKING OFF YOUR EXCUSES

Excuse #1 "I might need it one day"
Excuse Buster: "If I can't use it today, right now, for who I am in the life I am living, I don't need it. ('Just in case' keeps me from living in the present!)"

List here the things you "might need some day" and why you might need them. As you look at each item, say the Excuse Buster (yes, out loud) and see how it can change how you feel about the item.

_____   _____

_____   _____

_____   _____

Excuse #2 "It's too important to let go."
Excuse Buster: "If it is so important, then I must give it the honor and value it deserves (or let it go)."

List here the things that are "too important to let go" and why they are so important. As you look at each item, say the Excuse Buster (yes, out loud) and see how it can change how you feel about the item.

_____   _____

_____   _____

_____   _____

Excuse #3 "I can't get rid of it—it's worth a lot of money."
Excuse Buster: "I'm paying dearly now for the space and energy it is taking up in my home."

List here the things you're holding onto because "it's worth a lot of money" and also write down how much money you think each is really worth. Is it worth a lot because it's an antique or priceless item? Or is it worth a lot of money because you paid a lot of money for it once but have not used it since? Be honest with your answers. As you look at each item, say the Excuse Buster (yes, out loud) and see how it can change how you feel about the item.

_____   _____

_____   _____

_____   _____

Excuse #4 "It's not that I own too much stuff. It's just that my house is too small."
Excuse Buster: "I can't magically make my house bigger but I can reduce the number of things in my house."

You only have the space you have. If you are serious about your house being too small, write down why it is too small and the steps you can take to increase the size of your home or to acquire a new one. If, as I suspect, you are simply crowded out by stuff, write down the area(s) in your house that are most affected (these rooms are where you need to start the decluttering process).

My house is too small because _____.

_____

One step I can take toward acquiring a new home is _____.

_____

One step I can take toward increasing the room in my home is _____.

_____

My house feels smallest _____.

_____

Excuse #5 "I don't have the time."
Excuse Buster: "I give time to what I most value; my home and the relationships it nurtures should not be last on the list."

Time is a challenge, but how much time are you losing time by searching for keys, and bills, and clothes that fit, and clearing the kitchen counter before being able to cook. You know what I mean here.

Make a time commitment to your home and the life you want to live in it: Write down here how much time a day or a week you are willing to give to your home—then do it!

_____

_____

_____

CLUTTER STEALS TIME FROM YOUR LIFE

- How much time do you spend looking for your keys, or an unpaid bill, or the permission slip for your kid's field trip?
- Do you need to spend time clearing the kitchen counter just so you have a place to prepare meals? How about the kitchen or dining room tables—how long does it take to get them meal worthy? Or do you just give up and eat dinner in front of the TV?
- Does listening to a favorite CD involve searching through your disorganized music collection?
- Does setting up a place for your kids to make holiday decorations require moving piles and hunting fruitlessly for last year's long-lost supplies?
- Are your closets so crammed with clothes that you can't find anything to wear?

Excuse #6 "I don't know how it got like this."
Excuse Buster: "The source of the clutter isn't as important as committing to get rid of it."

Understanding how clutter came to live in your home is helpful, but what's important now is creating a clear plan and taking action to make it go away. Often it's tough to get stated decluttering your home or personal space. Consider for a moment what resources you might try to commit to this process—a friend, a family member, a professional organizer, and—of course—this workbook. Write down one resource you have to help you clear out clutter and get organized.

Excuse #7 "It's not a problem—my husband/wife/partner/child just thinks it is."
Excuse Buster: "I won't let clutter get between me and my relationships."

One family member is a pack rat; the others are not. If you have been labeled the pack rat, while it may not bother you (although I'm not so sure that really is true) it is having an effect on the family and something needs to change. Write here the biggest complaint your husband/wife/partner/child has about you as if it were about someone else and try to see the situation through their eyes. Is there something you can change?

_____

_____

_____

Excuse #8 "All this stuff isn't mine. I'm just holding it for someone"
Excuse Buster: "If it's not mine it goes back to where it belongs—pronto!"

Unless you are running a storage facility and getting paid for the privilege of holding onto other people's stuff it needs to go. It can be hard to tell someone to get their stuff out of your house (especially since you meant well by offering to keep it for them). Your home exists to create the life you want, not to store items that someone else won't take responsibility for.

First, make a list of things in your home that you're storing for other people and how long you've been holding onto them.

Item: Who I'm storing it for: How long it's been in my home:

_____

_____

_____

Now, write down here what you will say when you email them or call them to come and get their things. Give them a time frame and tell them what you will have to do with it if they can't pick it up.

_____

_____

_____

Excuse #9 "It's too overwhelming."
Excuse Buster: "I will take one step toward decluttering and break the big task into small pieces that I can handle."

You've taken the first step by honestly assessing the state of your home and committing to the decluttering program. Depending on the state of your home and the amount of clutter you are hoping to clear, this can be a big job. Sometimes it just gets to be overwhelming. If so, step back, take a deep breath, and give yourself a pat on the back for what you've already done. Then take a break. But don't let a break last too long.

Excuse #10 _____

Excuse Buster: _____

Here's where you get to fill in your own, particular excuse. Everyone who has clutter in their lives has a way of justifying it to themselves and to others. It's not unusual. Look around you. Some people manage to create order instead of chaos. They're not richer or less busy or better than you are. But they have made a clear, uncluttered home a priority in their and their family's lives. You too can do this. Some part of you isn't wholly satisfied with your life; otherwise you wouldn't be reading this book. The rewards of decluttering will far exceed your expectations. You will feel stronger, happier, clearer, and freer. It's time to quit making excuses. It's time to live the life you imagine for yourself. You can do it!

2

Your Home

THERE IS A REAL ESTATE EXPRESSION, "curb appeal," which essentially means the first impression of a house as seen from the street. Forget about the clutter inside for a minute, and go out and take a look at the outside of your house. Seriously. Now! Go do it! Close your eyes and think back to the first time you saw this house. What did you imagine your life in this home would be like? I'll venture a guess that overwhelming clutter and feeling stressed by that clutter were never part of your original dream.

While it may seem that getting organized is the answer to clutter, in reality the first step has nothing to do with "the stuff." We start by first asking you to clarify what you want *from* your home and the life you live in it. Answering those key questions will get you started on making your home a true reflection of your vision, ideals, and values:

- What dream does your home represent to you?

  _____

- Is it fulfilling that dream?

  _____

- What do you want *from* your home?

  _____

- Why did you buy or rent your home in the first place?

  _____

- What most excited you about your home?

  _____

- What features most appealed to you? Are they still the same now that you've lived here awhile?

  _____

- How did you imagine your life in this home?

  _____

- How old were you when you bought your home?

  _____

- How big was your family when you moved into this home?

_____

- Have family circumstances changed?

_____

- How did it feel the first day you moved in?

_____

- How long did that feeling last?

_____

- Do you ever walk into any rooms of your house and have that "new home" feeling?

_____

- Are there rooms you don't go into—ever?

_____

- How long have you lived in this home?

_____

- Have you done work on the house or apartment? What kind? Why? Are you happy with the result?

_____

_____

_____

_____

_____

- Is there work that needs to be done now?

_____

_____

- Why haven't you done it?

_____

_____

- What have you chosen to spend the money on instead?

_____

_____

_____

- Have you regularly maintained your home?

_____

- When was the last time you washed the windows?

_____

- Is your yard well maintained?

_____

- How is the garage? Can you easily park your car in it?

_____

- Is your home too big? Too small? Why?

_____

_____

_____

- If you could change anything about your home or your yard, what would it be?

_____

_____

_____

_____

A home is an emotional and financial investment. If your home needs repairs but you are spending your money on stuff you don't need and filling your home with clutter you are doing a disservice both to your family and your hard earned income. You shouldn't have a leaky roof and a closet full of clothes with the tags still on them. By the same token, if

EMOTIONAL BENEFITS

When your space is neat, clear, and free from clutter, you'll notice a change in the way you feel about your life and your relationships. Your rooms fulfill the functions you've chosen for them. Gathering places are comfortable for friends and family. Your bedroom is a romantic oasis. Enjoy the peace, pride, and satisfaction that come with living the life that you've chosen for yourself.

your house looks like a showplace on the outside, but a mess on the inside, you are not allocating your time and resources effectively to support your ideal home and create the life you want.

IMAGINE THE LIFE YOU WANT TO LIVE

Life is never perfect, but we all have unique visions of the lives we wish were ours. When clutter fills your home, not only does it block your space but it also blocks your vision.

Set aside some time to think about your ideal life. Be realistic here. I am not talking about suddenly marrying Prince William or starring in the next mega-blockbuster. I'm talking about a better life, but one that is within your reach. Do this in whatever way you best think through your problems: find a quiet moment to write ideas down, engage in some thinking time at the gym, schedule an hour in your planner to sit in solitude and think, or set aside time in bed before you fall asleep. The details may be slow in coming to your mind. This is not unusual but it is important to progress and worth the investment of some quiet time. The following questions may help you in thinking through what it is you want from the one life you have.

- How do you spend your time? What is a typical weekday and weekend day?

_____

- How do you feel when you are at home?

_____

- Does your home look the way you want it to look?

_____

- Does your home feel like a home to you?

_____

- How do you feel when you walk in the front door?

_____

- How do you want to feel when you walk in the front door?

_____

- How do family members feel when they come home? Don't fill this in for them—ask them how they feel.

_____

- How do they want to feel when they come home?

_____

- What is it about your home that makes it uniquely yours?

  _____

- What does your relationship look like?

  _____

- What does your career look like?

  _____

- How do you interact with your family?

  _____

- Do you entertain? How often?

  _____

- What do you accomplish in your home?

  _____

- Do you see yourself as high-powered, successful, and on top of things?

  _____

- What does that look like?

  _____

- Where do you find peace in your home?

_____

- Where do you play?

_____

- Where do you handle practical issues like bills, work, or homework?

_____

- Where is your sanctuary?

_____

YOUR VISION OF YOUR IDEAL HOME

A tool called a vision board can help you to clarify and make concrete how you want to see your ideal home. You can make a vision board on a large sheet of paper, poster board, a bulletin board, or in a notebook. It will be a place where you collect images (cut or torn from magazines, newspapers, or you can draw them yourself) of how you imagine your home. (Note: if you pull a photo of a kitchen or couch out of a magazine, it doesn't mean you must eventually have that exact kitchen or couch in your home. It's what those images represent to you that counts.)

Your image board can include colors, textures, drawings, photographs, or words that describe your home. You can cut words from advertisements or make a list of your own. Think about using words that express the overall feel of your home like *airy, open, inviting, modern, clean,* or *cozy.* You can use paint chip cards or fabric swatches or wallpaper samples. The idea is to get the colors, textures, and feel of each room captured on your vision board. If you make it concrete and are clear about what you want then it is more likely to happen.

You can divide your vision board into sections for each room, or you can create a board for each room in the house. Remember, a family lives in this home and the entire family needs to come together to help the home achieve the vision you all have for it.

The kids can have fun with this project and create their own vision boards for their rooms or other rooms in the home. They may come up with something that resembles an electronics filled amusement park but it will give you an opportunity to talk with them about what the true purpose of a room is, the importance of what we surround ourselves with on a daily basis, and prioritizing how we spend our money and our time to create the spaces we live in.

Remember, the house is for the whole family so it's essential to involve everyone at every step of the way. If people are involved in the process, they'll be committed to the outcome. Here are some questions to consider as a family. Choose those that will get the whole family discussing what they want from your home and shared spaces.

• Do you like how your home looks?

_____

• How would you describe your overall style (shabby chic, ultra modern, farmhouse, eclectic)?

_____

• Is your style a conscious choice, or something that just happened?

_____

- Is there a predominant color in your home? Do you love it?

_____

- Does your furniture "match"?

_____

- What does your master bedroom look like? What about the other bedrooms?

_____

- How do you feel when you are in your bedroom?

_____

- Is there room in your bedroom for you to sleep peacefully?

_____

- Is your kitchen sleek and modern or classic and homey?

_____

- How do you feel when you are in your kitchen?

_____

- Is your living room lived in or a showplace?

_____

• How do you feel when you are in your living room?

_____

• Are the kids' rooms stuffed to overflowing or is there room to grow?

_____

• Are the kids comfortable? Do they complain about their space(s)?

_____

• Does the front hallway welcome you when you arrive home after a tiring day?

_____

• Do you have a handy place for keys, coats, mail, backpacks, etc.?

_____

• Is your garage crammed to the rafters with everything *but* the car?

_____

• Can your family gather for meals, fun, or relaxation without the interference of piles of junk?

_____

• When was the last time you gathered for some family time?

_____

TIME BENEFITS OF BUSTING CLUTTER

Gone are the minutes and hours spent cursing yourself or blaming the dog for eating your homework. When everything has a place, getting ready in the morning takes less time. You won't be late. You won't forget important dates or arrive at a meeting without critical papers. Tax time is a breeze (except for the check-writing part). You will feel more relaxed, confident, and in control. Your time belongs to you, not your stuff.

Once you have an image of what you'd like your life and your home to be, take a walk around the rooms in your home. Don't worry, we'll get to clearing out the clutter. For now I want you to practice a new way of looking at your stuff and your space. For each room in the house you will need to determine:

- How do I feel when I enter this room?
- How do I or my family members *want* to feel when we enter this room?
- What is this room's function now?
- What is the function I want it to have?
- In order to serve its function, what furniture, contents, and open space should the room contain?
- Does each item in this room enhance and advance the vision I have for the life I want?
- What things in this room are standing in the way of my vision?

SEEING IS BELIEVING

Grab a pen. We are now going to go room by room and I want you to describe how each room is now and how you want it to be. This could be very hard work so you may want to break the work up into segments. Don't forget to look at your vision board before each room so you have a clear image in your mind of your vision for that space.

MASTER BEDROOM

What I see

Clothes on the bed

_____

_____

_____

What I'd like to see

Clothes in the closet, dresser, & hamper

_____

_____

_____

KID'S ROOMS

What I see

Toys & clothes on the floor

_____

_____

_____

What I'd like to see

The floor!

_____

_____

_____

FAMILY AND LIVING ROOMS

What I see

Books, bags, papers, toys
_____

_____

_____

What I'd like to see

Space to relax and enjoy movies, music,
and more
_____

_____

_____

HOME OFFICE

What I see

Piles of papers
_____

_____

_____

What I'd like to see

Clear space to work; papers filed
_____

_____

_____

KITCHEN

What I see

No place to prepare or eat food
_____

_____

_____

What I'd like to see

Clean counters
_____

_____

_____

DINING ROOM

What I see

Books, toys, papers, games

_____

_____

_____

What I'd like to see

An inviting table

_____

_____

_____

BATHROOM

What I see

Shampoos, soaps, products

_____

_____

_____

What I'd like to see

Stuff we really use

_____

_____

_____

GARAGE

What I see

Tools everywhere

_____

_____

_____

What I'd like to see

Tools arranged so I can find and use them

_____

_____

_____

BASEMENT

What I see

Boxes of old stuff _____

_____

_____

_____

What I'd like to see

Open, clean shelves, with clearly identified

storage _____

_____

_____

_____

Anything you wrote in the "What I'd like to see" column becomes a goal for that particular room. Keep these mind as you go through the rest of the process in this workbook. Below is an even broader list of the goals for each room. Really be specific here and take your time. Our goal is to identify your ideal vision—and that takes time and honesty. Oh, and let's be clear: This does not constitute an invitation to shop!

MASTER BEDROOM

Goal (What I'd Like to See) _____

_____

_____

_____

_____

KIDS' ROOMS

Goal (What I'd Like to See) _____

_____

_____

_____

_____

FAMILY AND LIVING ROOMS

Goal (What I'd Like to See) _____

_____

_____

_____

_____

HOME OFFICE

Goal (What I'd Like to See) _____

_____

_____

_____

_____

KITCHEN

Goal (What I'd Like to See) _____

_____

_____

_____

_____

DINING ROOM

Goal (What I'd Like to See) _____

_____

_____

_____

_____

BATHROOM

Goal (What I'd Like to See) _____

_____

_____

_____

_____

Goal (What I'd Like to See)

_____

_____

_____

_____

_____

THE HARD QUESTIONS

The key question you should ask yourself when looking at the clutter that fills your home is: **Does this item enhance and advance the vision I have for the life I want or does it impede that vision?**

Now that you're reflecting on the vision you have for the home you want and are thinking about the rooms in your house, it's time to ask some additional hard questions to deepen and broaden your thinking.

Answer each question by circling Yes or No:

- Are you weighed down by clutter?   Yes   No
- Do you own your stuff or does it own you?   Yes   No
- Does the clutter affect your emotions?   Yes   No
- Does the clutter affect your relationships?   Yes   No
- Does it affect your ability to socialize or entertain?   Yes   No
- Does it affect your children?   Yes   No
- Are your children happy in your home?   Yes   No
- Does the clutter affect your psychological and   Yes   No
  spiritual health?
- Does it affect your physical health?   Yes   No
- Does it affect your ability to succeed in your career?   Yes   No

Look carefully at your answers. If you have answered "Yes" more than twice, you have a clutter problem. If you're struggling with clutter, chances are that your lack of space is suffocating you. It doesn't leave enough air for you to live your life. Stuff alone doesn't make you happy and when it becomes "too much" it separates you from what you want and who you love. Stuff can very easily become the major hurdle that traps you in a miserable and unsatisfying life rather than assisting you to live the life you truly want. I have seen it time and again—if you open your space, you open your life to infinite possibilities. Time to get that space clear!

3

Putting Clutter in Its Place

WE'RE GOING TO GET DOWN to a room-by-room, step-by-step analysis of what to toss and what to keep, but to get the whole household warmed up, I like to start by doing a high-speed, low-level purge, otherwise known as the Kick Start.

As you launch your Kick Start, keep in mind that you'll do it F.A.S.T:

Fix a time—schedule a time and make it happen.
Anything not used for twelve months—out the door!
Someone else's stuff—return it or get rid of it!
Trash—gone forever!

There are three categories for the things you encounter in your kick start purge.

1. Keep
- This is the stuff that you want, use, and is critical to the life you want to live.
- Or (let's be honest) stuff you don't really use but can't bear to part with just now.

2. Trash/recycle
- Every bag you fill represents space you've created to live and love your life.
- Everything you decide to get rid of is a victory.
- Make it a competition to see who can fill more trash/recycle bags.

3. Out the door
- Sell—at a yard sale, on consignment, or online.
- Donate to a charitable organization (see Resources section).
- Return things to their rightful owners or give to someone who has a real use for that item.

Plan where you're going to sort your belongings. If you have the space, put three tarps on the lawn labeled "keep," "trash/recycle," and "out the door." If you don't have outdoor space or it's too cold, create defined spaces for each pile by spreading sheets indoors. Don't have room to spread the sheets? Create "keep" and "out the door" areas in the middle of the room you're working on and box it up as you go. Everything for the trash or recycling goes immediately outside.

CLUTTER CONFLICT RESOLUTION

If there is more than one person in your family you may not reach an immediate agreement on what to keep, trash/recycle, or donate. Most likely there will be discussion about how to sort items. When talking with your family, sometimes it's not what you say, but how you say it. Remember that your family members are more important than all the stuff. It's helpful to focus on what an item means to you or represents, then you have a much better chance of clearly communicating your need to have something in your home. A key to making progress here is to keep in mind

COMMUNICATION QUESTIONS

Here are some questions to help you make decisions about what to keep without starting arguments or passing judgment. The goal is to reframe the discussion away from the item itself to its significance in your lives.

EXAMPLES

1. Instead of "Why don't you put your tools away?" ask "What is it that you want from this space?"
2. Instead of "Why do we have to keep your grandmother's sewing kit?" ask "Why is that important to you? Does it have meaning?"
3. Instead of "There's no room for all of your stuff in there," say "Let's see how we can share this space so that it works for all of us."
4. Instead of "Why do you have to hold onto these ugly sweaters your dad gave you?" ask "What do these sweaters make you think of or remind you of?"
5. Instead of saying "I don't understand how you can live with all of this junk," ask "How do you feel when you have to spend time in this room?"

your vision as well as constantly working to understand someone else's need to keep his or her items.

This quick purge is just a primer. But it will fill you with excitement and a real sense of what you can achieve. After you're done you'll see immediate results. Though this one time through won't completely reconfigure your house, you should be proud. You've done a good job clearing away the first level of clutter, and now you're ready to tackle the real issues.

Hash it out

Remember, the use and function of a room should be determined by how you want that room to be used. You should be making conscious choices regarding the furniture, the activities that will take place in the space, and who will be using it. At the beginning of this process you took a closer look at your rooms to see what was really there. That evaluation started you thinking about how you want each room to be. Do you want to go to sleep in a bedroom that makes you feel relaxed and comfortable? Do you want to have dinner in a dining room that can be romantic or alive with family dynamics? Do you want to work in a home office that makes you feel efficient and on top of things? This process is taking your vision for your life and making it a reality.

IT'S A FAMILY AFFAIR

Unless you live alone, you will need to communicate and come to a consensus on how each area in the home is to be used and valued. Those who share your home should have an opportunity to define their vision as well as speak openly about the life they want and the things they wish to surround themselves with. The vision boards you created are a great jumping-off point for your discussion about the overall feel and look and function each of you envisions for your home.

- What is our vision

Self _____

Spouse/Partner _____

Child _____

Child _____

Child _____

- How do we imagine using the space?

Self _____

Spouse/Partner _____

Child _____

Child _____

Child _____

- What is the intersection of our different visions and lives?

_____

_____

_____

- How can we make it work for everyone?

_____

_____

_____

- As parents, are you setting the tone and defining the vision or are you giving equal voice to the children?

_____

_____

_____

Ask each family member to think about how they imagine using the spaces in your home. In common areas (living room, kitchen/dining room) there may be conflicting ideas about the best use for the space. Use common sense. In areas like the master bedroom you can obviously pull rank if your kids want to use it as a game room. However, if they have certain ideas for their own rooms, it pays to listen. Maybe it's time for the Winnie the Pooh theme to go, now that Junior is older. You may still be seeing your "baby" while your child is growing up.

IF YOU LIVE ALONE

If you are king or queen of your castle then you get to make all the decisions about how a space in your home will be used. Sounds good, right? Not always. Sometimes it can be difficult to come to a decision about your stuff without bringing in another perspective. Can you enlist the help of a friend, neighbor, or family member? Your sister who prides herself on being organized might be more than happy to come over and help you with your closet. You may not need someone with you for working on the whole house or apartment, but it could help immensely to choose a room, get another pair of eyes (and hands!) working on it and get the clutter out.

You'll be surprised by what this process opens up for you and your family, how it forces you to reevaluate your feelings about what you own and what you perceive as important. In fact, you can expect some degree of surprise, confusion, and even conflict in this process. I have frequently found that although people may share a common living space, their individual ideas or visions for that space can vary enormously. However, it is possible to coordinate your visions for the spaces in your home, manage the clutter, and decide *together* what really belongs and what does not.

ROOM FUNCTION CHARTS

It's important to get agreement on the function of each room. To do so, each family member will need a copy of the Room Function Chart for each room of the house (see Appendix for a blank chart you can duplicate). Fill them out individually, then get together to compare your results. You might want to set aside a weekend morning or afternoon to allow time to complete the charts and be able to discuss them.

The following questions can inspire conversation that will help you find common ground when you fill out the Room Function Chart.

- What do you like most about this room?

_____

_____

- What stresses you out the most about this room?

_____

_____

- How would you like to feel when you walk into this space?

  _____

  _____

- What do you need from this space?

  _____

  _____

- What do you want your friends to see when they come into this room?

  _____

  _____

- What do you wish someone else in the family would fix in this room?

  _____

  _____

- What do you think you should fix in this room?

  _____

  _____

- What will be the hardest thing to fix/change in this room?

  _____

  _____

- What will help you to achieve what you'd like for this room?

_____

_____

- How can you help others achieve their goals for this room?

_____

_____

ROOM FUNCTION CHART	
MASTER BEDROOM	
Current function	
Ideal function	
Who uses it?	
Who should use it?	
What should it contain?	
What has to go?	
KID'S ROOM	
Current function	
Ideal function	
Who uses it?	
Who should use it?	

What should it contain?	
What has to go?	
FAMILY/LIVING ROOM	
Current function	
Ideal function	
Who uses it?	
Who should use it?	
What should it contain?	
What has to go?	
HOME OFFICE	
Current function	
Ideal function	
Who uses it?	
Who should use it?	
What should it contain?	
What has to go?	
KITCHEN	
Current function	
Ideal function	
Who uses it?	

Who should use it?	
What should it contain?	
What has to go?	
DINING ROOM	
Current function	
Ideal function	
Who uses it?	
Who should use it?	
What should it contain?	
What has to go?	
BATHROOM	
Current function	
Ideal function	
Who uses it?	
Who should use it?	
What should it contain?	
What has to go?	
GARAGE	
Current function	
Ideal function	

Who uses it?	
Who should use it?	
What should it contain?	
What has to go?	
BASEMENT	
Current function	
Ideal function	
Who uses it?	
Who should use it?	
What should it contain?	
What has to go?	
Complete these questions for each room in the house you are decluttering.	

No one is a mind reader. When visions for a shared space are openly discussed everyone has an opportunity to voice their views. In this way criteria can be agreed upon for what is kept and what is let go. Chances are that everyone has an opinion—even some very strong ones. If there are multiple visions for one room, you need to lay out the particulars so you can determine how that room can be best used to serve the entire family.

Conflicting visions

Often there will be one room in the house that each family member has a strong opinion about—typically a spare room or the living/family room.

In the following space write the name of the room in question and each person's vision for it:

Room: _____

Self: _____

Spouse/Partner: _____

Child: _____

Child: _____

Child: _____

Discuss what the family needs most. Is a home office critical to supporting the family? Is the dining room the best place for social gathering? Is there a mother-in-law who makes frequent visits and needs a place to stay? Does a hobby deserve the space it consumes or is the scrapbooking and crafting a fantasy that will never come true?

How will this room be used now?

_____

What does it need to achieve this ideal function?

_____

Who will be responsible for making it happen?

_____

Multipurposes

Often the problem isn't that family members disagree—it's that the room needs to serve more than one function. The recreation room in the basement is the "only" place to store family heirlooms. The office *has* to double as a guest room. First, consider whether these multiple uses of a space are reasonable or just an excuse to avoid making a decision about the clutter. On the other hand, having an office that doubles as a guest room is not uncommon or unreasonable. Look for ways to make purposes overlap. Replace a bed with a sleep sofa. Use a file cabinet that doubles as a nightstand.

There has to be some compromise. Some decisions will be made on the basis of what is best for the whole family. This can be difficult, but if the whole family is involved there is a greater chance of everyone accepting the outcome. And remember—just because you're the parent, doesn't mean what you say automatically goes!

COMMON GOALS

The family needs to sit down together to discuss the individual room charts each family member completed for each room in the house. You set aside an afternoon to fill out the charts; maybe you should set aside a weeknight to pull them out and go over them together. It will be illuminating to see where your visions overlap and where they are in conflict. I bet you will all learn something new about each other.

If you are in conflict over the use of a space, then each family member needs to make his or her case about the use of a room. It's important that everyone have an opportunity to speak (and listen!) and that you determine together not only the overall function of your home but the function of each of the rooms within it.

When you come to an agreement on common goals, start filling out a Room Function Chart that best combines everyone's ideas and comments. The complete chart should look something like this:

Sample COMPLETED ROOM FUNCTION CHART	
MASTER BEDROOM	
Current function	Mom and dad's bedroom, laundry transition site, and kid book reading and family DVD-watching central.
Ideal function	Peace and quiet! Sleep!
Who uses it now?	Kids read in here every night before bed. Everyone watches movies together.
Who should use it?	Mom & Dad only! From now on we watch the movies in the family room.
What should it contain?	Our bed, our clothes, our personal items.
What has to go?	Everything that is not Mom & Dad specific.
KID'S ROOM	
Current function	Sleep, toys, play, music, TV, computer games.
Ideal function	Sleep, homework, rest, relaxation.
Who uses it?	Kids.
Who should use it?	Kids.
What should it contain?	Bed, desk, dresser, bookshelf books, toys.
What has to go?	Broken or unused toys, outgrown toys, clothes and books and —TV?

FAMILY ROOM	
Current function	TV and movie watching, homework room, exercise room, game room, library, dining room, craft room.
Ideal function	Family TV and movie watching, game room.
Who uses it?	Everyone.
Who should use it?	Everyone.
What should it contain?	Couch, chairs and tables free of piles, storage for DVDs, games, and books. Clear floor space.
What has to go?	Crafts center, exercise equipment, eating dinner in here.
FORMAL LIVING ROOM	
Current function	Bill-paying and storage for dad's sports memorabilia and mom's boxes of collectibles.
Ideal function	Formal entertaining.
Who uses it?	Dad and Mom.
Who should use it?	Everyone.
What should it contain?	Couch, chairs and tables free of piles. Clear floor space.
What has to go?	Sports memorabilia. And we need to make room in the office so dad can pay the bills in there.
KITCHEN	
Current function	Where we cook and eat.
Ideal function	The same as above.

Who uses it?	Everyone.
Who should use it?	Everyone.
What should it contain?	Food, dishes, cooking supplies.
What has to go?	Too many cooking supplies that we don't use. It's too hard to cook and keep things clean.

DINING ROOM

Current function	A place where the kids play, do their homework, and keep their school supplies.
Ideal function	A place where the family gathers to eat together. It'd also be nice to have dinner parties now and then!
Who uses it?	The kids.
Who should use it?	Everyone.
What should it contain?	The dining table and chairs, clutter-free, and room to walk around the table.
What has to go?	The toys! And homework supplies. But where?

BATHROOM

Current function	Bathing, showering.
Ideal function	Same as above.
Who uses it?	Everyone.
Who should use it?	Everyone.
What should it contain?	Basics of shampoo, conditioner, soap.

What has to go?	Travel-size bottles, old soaps, ragged towels. Stained rugs, outdated medicines.
BASEMENT	
Current function	Storage of who-knows-what.
Ideal function	Storage for seasonal decorations, furniture, and exercise equipment; possibly a family play room.
Who uses it?	Everyone.
Who should use it?	Everyone.
What should it contain?	Clearly labeled storage areas and cartons; exercise equipment that is used; dad's tools.
What has to go?	Boxes of old books, clothes, junk, other people's tools and possessions, high school and college possessions, broken toys.
GARAGE	
Current function	Storage of everything—who knows?
Ideal function	Keep car, yard equipment, seasonal sports equipment.
Who uses it?	Everyone.
Who should use it?	Everyone.
What should it contain?	Car, places for tools (if not in basement), gardening stuff, seasonal sports equipment.
What has to go?	Boxes of old books, clothes, junk, other people's stuff.

We're going to work our way up from bottom to top of the function chart because to make way for the new, we need to pay close attention to the old.

Example:

ROOM:	WHAT HAS TO GO:
Master bedroom	*The TV and the DVD collection.*
Kid's room	*Broken or unused toys; outgrown toys, clothes, and books (stuffed animals).*
Living room	*Sports memorabilia.*
	Make room in the office so Dad can pay the bills in there.
Home office	*Magazines, unused scrapbooking materials.*
Kitchen	*Too many unused cooking supplies.*
	It's hard to cook and keep things clean.
Dining room	*The toys.*
Bathroom	*Travel-size bottles, old soaps, ragged towels.*
Garage	*Boxes of old books, clothes, junk, other people's tools and possessions.*

Now it is your turn:

ROOM:	WHAT HAS TO GO:
Master bedroom	

Kid's room

_____

_____

_____

Family/
living room

_____

_____

Home office

_____

_____

_____

Kitchen

_____

_____

Dining room

_____

_____

Bathroom

_____

_____

Garage

_____

_____

_____

"What has to go" becomes your to-do list for preparing that room for change. By focusing on specific types of clutter, you can drill a little deeper here to get closer to your vision for the room in question.

ONE ROOM'S CLUTTER IS STILL ANOTHER ROOM'S CLUTTER

Going room by room shouldn't be an exercise in redistributing clutter from one place to another. This is yet another opportunity to use your **Kick Start** tools of keep, trash/recycle, and out the door. If there are too many toys in the dining room, it's time to (1) trash the toys that are broken or missing pieces; (2) sell or give away the toys that work but that the kids have outgrown or no longer play with; and (3) keep the toys that they currently enjoy. Once you have vetted the toys they can go into the kids' rooms. Be aware that you may need to do another purge when you are working on each kid's room.

The column "what should it contain" becomes a checklist for what you may need to add or take away to complete your vision of that room.

ROOM: WHAT IT SHOULD CONTAIN:

Master bedroom
_____
_____
_____

Kid's room
_____
_____
_____

Family/
living room _____

_____

_____

Home office _____

_____

_____

Kitchen _____

_____

_____

Dining room _____

_____

_____

Bathroom _____

_____

_____

Garage _____

_____

_____

_____

If you don't have the appropriate tools you can't effectively use the space for its intended purposes. Each area that has a specific purpose within a room will be called a zone.

IDENTIFY SPECIFIC ZONES WITHIN ROOMS

Rooms are used for different purposes—often at the same time. You need to identify the different activities that take place within each room. Thinking about rooms in terms of zones or activities both helps you keep clutter at bay and helps you understand how you use your spaces. Then you can match the zones with "What should it contain" to see if you have the items that can help you to fulfill the purpose of the zone and the room.

Example:

MASTER BEDROOM	ITEM	HAVE OR NEED?
Sleeping	bed	Have
Relaxation	armchair	Need
Clothes	dresser	Need
	closet	Have
Shoes	closet	Have
Off-season clothes and shoes	storage	Need
Reading	good light/lamp	Need

Your turn:

MASTER BEDROOM	ITEM	HAVE OR NEED?
Sleeping		
Relaxation		
Clothes		

MASTER BEDROOM (CONT.)	ITEM	HAVE OR NEED?
Shoes	_____	_____
Off-season clothes and shoes	_____	_____
Reading	_____	_____

KID'S BEDROOM

Sleeping	_____	_____
Clothes	_____	_____
Shoes	_____	_____
Homework	_____	_____
Toys	_____	_____
Reading	_____	_____
Crafts	_____	_____
Music	_____	_____

FAMILY/LIVING ROOM

Media—music and video/DVD	_____	_____
Reading	_____	_____
Games	_____	_____
Collectibles	_____	_____
Relaxation	_____	_____
Photos	_____	_____
Storage	_____	_____

HOME OFFICE	*ITEM*	*HAVE OR NEED?*
Bill paying	_____	_____
Reading	_____	_____
Studying	_____	_____
Computer work	_____	_____
Mail	_____	_____
Files	_____	_____
Scrapbooking	_____	_____
Crafting	_____	_____

KITCHEN		
Preparation	_____	_____
Cooking	_____	_____
Cleanup	_____	_____
Eating	_____	_____
Storage	_____	_____

DINING ROOM		
Storage	_____	_____
Eating	_____	_____
Collectibles	_____	_____
Formal china	_____	_____
Entertaining supplies	_____	_____

BATHROOM	ITEM	HAVE OR NEED?
Cleaning supplies	_____	_____
Personal products	_____	_____
Extra products	_____	_____
Shared products	_____	_____
Medicine	_____	_____

GARAGES, BASEMENTS, AND OTHER STOREROOMS		
Garden supplies	_____	_____
Laundry	_____	_____
Tools	_____	_____
Paint and chemicals	_____	_____
Sporting gear	_____	_____
Seasonal decorations	_____	_____
Workbench	_____	_____

Some items will be used for more than one zone. For example, a child's desk could be a place where she does homework as well as crafts. It's important that school books and crafting supplies are not in chaos within that zone so you may need to create separate sections in each zone. Never have more than two functions set up for one zone. If you have too many zones fighting for too little space you will find the clutter increasing and obscuring the purpose of the zone.

BEFORE YOU SHOP—REPURPOSE!

One caveat here: The "need" items list *is not* a license to go out and buy furniture, appliances, and what-have-you. See it as an opportunity to repurpose things that are already in your home. That lamp from your Aunt Matilda may not fit the décor in your living room but with a new shade it might be perfect in your bedroom. That chair you're always tripping over in the living room could work as seating in the reading corner in the bedroom. No longer need the kids' toy chest? Could you refinish it, put it at the end of your bed, and use it for storage of off-season clothing? Look around your home and rooms with new eyes and you might discover new uses for old items.

Shelving and storage

While you are figuring out what fits where, there is a concrete way to measure your space for what it can contain. I've said it before: You can't fit four cubic feet of stuff into two cubic feet of space and not have clutter. So get out your tape measure and see what will work in the space you have.

First, measure your shelving space or bookshelves or hanging space and use the table below to work out how many of a particular item will fit. Then sort your belongings until you get to a number you know will comfortably fit into that space. If you're feeling ambitious, get rid of even more so you'll have room to grow. Also, if you need to put up shelves to get the books, DVDs, and so on off of the floor or out of boxes, you will know how much shelving will fit your needs.

As you draw up your plans for each room, let math be your guide. What's physically possible for the space? Measure the total length of your bookshelves. How much linear footage for books do you actually have?

MATH OF STUFF CHEAT SHEET	
ITEM	NUMBER THAT WILL FIT INTO ONE LINEAR FOOT OF SPACE
VHS tapes	11
DVD cases	20
CDs in jewel cases	29
Magazine box with 10 magazines	3 (30 magazines total)
Books	12 (on average)
Jeans / pants	12
Shirts / blouses	15
Heavy jackets / suits	6
Shoes	Estimate about 8 inches per pair.

How many books will fit there? What is the hanging space you have available? Assess how many items will hang in that space so you know what to discard. You need to assess your space limitations and design accordingly. This will also help take some of the emotion out of the discussion. You only have the space you have!

GETTING READY TO GO ROOM BY ROOM

Now we're going to make that Room Function Chart a reality by working through your house, room by room.

A NOTE FOR APARTMENT DWELLERS

If you live in an apartment or condo your needs for space are a bit different from someone who lives in a house. Rooms in an apartment often need to serve multiple purposes. One closet houses your current clothing but also serves as storage for seasonal clothes. Your kitchen table may need to be used for eating, crafting, bill paying, and homework. The key to solving the zone and space overlap is to designate storage and usage for the purposes you need each room to serve. For example, crafting material can be kept in a storage container that comes out when you do your crafting in the kitchen and is put away to make way for dinner. Homework supplies can be put in a small drawer in the kitchen (pencils, sharpener, scissors, ruler, and eraser) and brought out when needed and put away when done. A homework supply drawer would be a much, much better use of space than a junk drawer in your kitchen! Who wants to keep junk around anyway?

If homework supplies aren't a necessity in your home then you can use this drawer as a mini-toolbox. Keep a screwdriver, small hammer, scissors, tape, nails and screws for small repairs around the apartment. It's also a great place for a flashlight and extra batteries.

THE GROUND RULES

No matter what the size of your home, for every room you approach, there are three critical steps.

1. Think it through
What's particular to that room in terms of the stuff that needs to be in it, the stuff that tends to accumulate in it, and how you're going to approach the task.

2. Set it up

Refer to your Room Function Chart.

Establish zones for the different activities that take place in the room

Figure out what doesn't belong in the room.

3. Make it happen

This is the action plan that will help you make your vision for the space a reality.

You have done a lot of hard thinking about what is in your home and the ideal purpose it should serve. Remember, stuff seems to accumulate on its own but in reality the only way it comes into our homes is if we give it permission to enter. Say "no" to stuff and "yes" to a home and life the way you want to live it. In the next few chapters you will be looking at the rooms in your home in an extreme close-up. I'll be asking you to write down much of what you discover. Not only does writing it down allow you to stop and focus on what you are seeing and doing, it will help you to clarify what is already in your space and what you really want it to be like. Pencils ready? Let's go!

4

The Master Bedroom

YOU SHOULD HAVE HIT the master bedroom on your quick purge of the house. It felt good, didn't it? Clearing out spaces and making room for the things you value is like a breath of fresh air for both you and the spaces you live in. And if a surface clean can put a smile on your face, imagine the grins and joy that a real nitty-gritty decluttering will bring!

Your bedroom should be a space that reflects your vision of your relationship and fosters calm, warmth, and love. Remember, too, that we all have a relationship with ourselves and the responsibility that comes with that relationship is to be sure we are healthy, well-rested, and have a place to find peace and quiet. No matter what the status of your personal life you owe it to yourself to create a haven for yourself in your home. The master bedroom is that haven.

Write down your responses to the following questions and have your partner do the same, then compare your answers. You may be surprised what you find out about each other.

- How do I feel when I enter my bedroom?

_____

- How do I *want* to feel when we enter this room?

_____

- What is standing in the way of that feeling?

_____

- What is this room's function (or functions) now?

_____

- What is the function I want it to have?

_____

- What is my favorite part of this room?

_____

- What do I really dislike? Can I change that part of the room?

_____

- In order to serve its ideal function, what furniture, contents, and open space should the room contain?

Furniture: _____

Contents: _____

Open space: _____

- What is on the walls? Photos? Paintings? Nothing? (Are they still waiting to be hung?)

_____

- Has your bedroom become a storage area?

_____

- Do you wake up in the morning feeling more tired than when you went to bed?

_____

- Do your kids use it as their media center or playroom?

_____

- Are your crafts and scrapbooking projects threatening to take over?

_____

- Are you able to keep the room clean and ordered?

_____

• Is your closet so full you can't find what you need to get dressed in the morning?

_____

• Does each item in this room enhance and advance the vision you have for the life you want?

_____

• What else is happening in this room that might be adding to the clutter?

_____

THINK IT THROUGH

The master bedroom is *your* space. Get rid of the kids' video games, old toys or clothing. The kids have the rest of the house; the master bedroom should be off limits to them. You need to create a space for just you, the grown-up, where you relax and restore yourself. It's a space for you and your partner to enjoy. Focus on what you want from this space and keep that vision clearly in mind as we clear the clutter, organize what should belong in the space, and set the tone for your serene getaway from the cares and hassles of daily life! This is the fundamental reason for getting organized—to live a richer, fuller, and more rewarding life. Get to it!

SET IT UP

Now, let's take a minute and pull together all the hard work and thought you have put into envisioning your ideal master bedroom. Write it down here as a touchstone for the work you are about to do to get this room in shape.

Goals (from page 31): _____

Ideal function (from page 45): _____

What has to go (from page 55): _____

_____

What it should contain (from page 57): _____

_____

MAKE IT HAPPEN

Consider increasing those aspects of the master bedroom that add to it being a room for grown-ups and discarding anything that doesn't enhance the idea of an adult retreat and haven. This is the place where you are most intimate with your partner, together building a deep and lasting sexual and personal relationship. This is where you sleep, and one of the most important aspects of health is getting good restful sleep. This is where you relax away from the day-to-day cares of the family and the home. This is the place where you get ready everyday to face the world and where you come to decompress at the end of the day. Your bedroom should function as a haven and your closet should be set up so you can dress efficiently every morning. I promise that the calm you create in this space will be returned many times over.

While you are focusing on your bedroom, take a look around and see if it needs a fresh coat of paint. Since you will be clearing out the clutter from your drawers and closets and under your bed you are already halfway to cleaning the room from top to bottom. Now's a good time to assess the state of things underneath the clutter. Take a look at the floor-

THE MASTER BEDROOM IS THE HEART OF YOUR RELATIONSHIP

No room in a home should be more important to a couple than their bedroom. Disarray in this room has more impact on family life, on peace and harmony, and on a relationship than it does in any other room. Your bedroom is the most private room in your house and it reflects how you value yourself and your relationship. Sometimes because it is private, it's tempting to hide your mess behind closed doors. But don't forget that the bedroom is the scene of your most intimate, vulnerable moments. Letting it be overrun with conflicting functions will inevitably take a toll on your psyche and your relationship.

ing or carpet and see if that should be replaced or deep cleaned. You don't want to go through the effort of sorting your clothes only to return them to a less than clean closet or a broken drawer. Nor do you want to go through the effort of making your master bedroom a haven that has dingy walls or peeling wallpaper.

The bed and your clothes can stay—everything else goes

You heard me: the bed and your clothes. That's it. It's very simple. Sleeping, dressing, and nurturing your relationship are the primary functions of the master bedroom. Anything that can't be considered "bed" or "clothes" doesn't have a place in your bedroom. Out it goes.

Just as the kitchen represents the heart of your home and nourishes, your master bedroom represents the heart of you and your relationship and drives the emotional mood of your home. In order to create a sense of calm and well-being for you, your family, and your entire home, you need to commit to getting your master bedroom in order. Imagine the room clean and set up to be an area for you to relax and recover from your day.

- Remember your vision for this room. How does what's in the room now serve that vision? List the things that fulfill that vision here:

_____

_____

_____

- What takes away from it? List those things here:

_____

_____

_____

Clear out everything that doesn't truly belong. This means toys, papers, boxes, broken items needing to be repaired, and hobby supplies. In other words, anything that is not sleeping or dressing related. Don't forget to get the owners of these piles involved. The kids need to reclaim their toys, dad needs to get his model plane off the dresser—you get the idea. This is not just an exercise in reallocating clutter—all of these items will be dealt with in their appropriate places and rooms.

MAPPING YOUR ZONES

The critical zones in most bedrooms are the same: sleeping, relaxing, dressing, and storing clothes, shoes, and accessories.

Remember when we talked about the tools or items (furniture, storage) that allow you to maximize your zones? Well here's when we're

THE SANCTITY OF THE BEDROOM

Naturally, it can be tempting to keep things in your bedroom that don't serve its function. Maybe it's the only place in your house where you have room for a desk. It may not be ideal, but it's practical. I respect your realism . . . but no. I have to put my foot down. Put your relationship first. Preserve your sense of peace. Deepen your intimacy. Enhance your sleep. Find another place for the desk. Even if you live in a studio apartment, you must create a separate, sacred space for your bedroom. Put up a screen or a curtain. Use a bookshelf to create a wall if you can't afford to have one built. This rule is too important to ignore.

going to take a close look at each zone, what's in it, and how to reduce the clutter and make it match your vision.

The master bedroom zones:

- Sleeping.
- Dressing.
- Storage for clothes, shoes, accessories, and off-season garb.
- Relaxing.

SLEEPING

Your bed is for rest and romance and is a reflection of your relationship with your spouse. If you do not have a partner, your bed is a space that welcomes you at the end of the day and offers a comfortable good night's sleep. If the bed is covered with laundry, toys, videos, and more it's not keeping to your vision of your room or your relationship or yourself. If you can't easily find your way to your bed, how can you find your way to

ROMANCE ENHANCER

Think back to your most romantic moments. Were you on vacation? At a spa? On your honeymoon? Is there something about that time or place that you can bring into your current bedroom? Think of a scent, a texture, or sound that brings you back to that place of romance and peace. Write below what you can incorporate into your bedroom to remind you of that time and enhance your romance.

_____

_____

connecting with your partner? Or, how can you simply find your way to getting peaceful sleep? Make your bed comfortable, inviting, or luxurious but make it your own.

Your bed

You must make your bed every day, without fail. Making your bed helps enormously to create an inviting place for rest, relaxation, and romance by creating a constantly organized and clean area. Now, let's take an inventory of what's on your bed before you make it. Do you have clothes and books and magazines that shouldn't be there? Time to get rid of them. And when I say "get rid of them" I don't mean stuff them into a drawer or another room. I mean really get rid of them.

Now let's look at the bed and see what's getting in your way to peaceful restful sleep.

Is your bed inviting?

_____

Is it a bed you want to slip into every night?

_____

Are the sheets clean?

_____

Are your pillows fluffy or is the stuffing lumpy and old?

_____

When was the last time you cleaned your comforter?

_____

Is your bed a haven for you and your partner? What would it take to make it one?

_____

Are the mattress and box spring still comfortable? Or is it time to replace them?

_____

Is your bed overrun with pillows that need to be removed every night? Why? Do you really need them? What purpose are they serving?

_____

Can you easily get into your bed? Are there boxes or tables or piles on the floor getting in your way?

Don't underestimate the effect a good night's sleep can have on your mood, your productivity, your health, and all of your relationships. The right pillow, a comfortable mattress, and cozy sheets can help you get the rest you need.

What's under the bed?

Look under the bed in your master bedroom. Traditional *feng shui* teaches that it is extremely bad for energy flow to be blocked by having something under the bed.

Drag everything that's under the bed out to the middle of the room. I bet those storage boxes didn't come out alone! It turns out there are actually monsters under most beds—in the form of allergy-causing dust and worse: dust mites. This isn't healthy and it's not necessary. Now, I know that some homes are smaller than others. When space is at a premium you tend to stash stuff wherever you can find space, but I really have to be clear here about putting things under the bed. Whatever is down there doesn't belong there. And before you put something down there, ask yourself: "Why am I holding onto this?" "Do I really need it?" If you do need it, then get it out and use it. If you don't, bag it up and throw it in the trash or recycle bin.

Out of sight is not out of mind. If you want your master bedroom to be a sanctuary and a haven for you and your partner then you have to make sure that includes the areas that you can't see.

DRESSING

Other than rest and romance, the master bedroom is the place where you get ready to meet the day. Whether you are putting on a business suit or a

THE MONSTERS UNDER (AND IN) YOUR BED

House dust mites are microscopic bugs that primarily live on dead skin cells regularly shed from humans and pets. Dust mites are harmless to most people. They don't carry diseases, but they can cause allergic reactions in asthmatics and others who are allergic to their feces.

A typical mattress may have anywhere from 100,000 to 10 million mites inside. Ten percent of the weight of a two-year-old pillow can be composed of dead mites and their droppings. Nearly 100,000 mites can live in one square yard of carpet.

WHAT CAN YOU DO?

Change bedding weekly.
Enclose your mattress and pillows in a plastic bed cover.
Wash all bedding in hot water.
Avoid feather pillows and choose synthetic materials.
Vacuum the box spring and around the base of the bed.

track suit you need to have a clear space where you can find the clothes you need and want to wear.

Your closet

Depending on what's in your closet, clearing it out will take between two and four hours, so set aside time when your energy will be full so that you can devote yourself to the task and get this done right. Remember this time is a commitment to you and your vision of your ideal life.

Let's start with the closet. Remember when you looked at your home from the curb and envisioned your dream for your life in it? I want you to take a look at your closet with that same perspective.

- When you open your closet door, what do you feel? Panic? Guilt? Confusion? Depression? Other emotions?

_____

- When you get dressed in the morning, how long does it take you?

_____

- If you can't get dressed quickly, is it because you aren't good at making decisions or because you can't find anything in the jumble of clothing that's in your way?

_____

- How many items of clothing do you have hanging in your closet that don't fit you?

_____

- Are you holding onto "vintage" clothes, i.e., the stuff you wore in college?

_____

- How many articles of clothing still have tags on them or are smothered in dry cleaning wrap?

_____

- Can you see the back of your closet?

_____

- If you needed to grab a pair of slacks that fit you, look good, and are clean, can you do it?

_____

Once your closet is empty of clothing and shoes, take the opportunity to give it a good clean—and paint if needed. Assess if you need new shelves or better lighting. Determine what storage aids you will need to maintain the space and enable you to easily get what you need when you need it. But don't think of creating space to store more stuff you will never use or wear.

As with much of the problem of clutter, we don't always see what is right in front of us. Are you pushing through clothes you haven't worn in years to get to the one or two pairs of trousers that fit? It's time to really see what is in your closet. Take everything out, arrange it in piles on your bed by article and count each item. Let's be honest and include the color too because I am sure you have more than one black sweater! And while you are being honest, put your current size here _____. Once you have

SEEING DOUBLE (OR TRIPLE OR MORE) IN THE CLOSET

A couple of years ago I was helping a man tame his closets. When we had sorted all of his clothes we discovered that he had twenty-two nearly identical pairs of khaki pants. He had so many clothes in his closet that he simply forgot what he had purchased and so each time he saw a pair of multipurpose dress-up or dress-down khakis he snapped them up. Twenty-two times!

Clothing	How many?	Color(s)	Size(s)
Example: Shirts	15	White cotton	8
		White silk	10
		Green Oxford	10
		Blue silk	10
		Blue + white cotton	12
Shirts/blouses	_____	_____	_____
Pants	_____	_____	_____
Jeans	_____	_____	_____
Work dresses	_____	_____	_____
Party dresses	_____	_____	_____
Jackets	_____	_____	_____
Suits	_____	_____	_____
Skirts	_____	_____	_____
Sweaters	_____	_____	_____

made your list, go back and put a circle around the items that you have worn in the last six months.

Are you shocked or amazed at the numbers? Do you have more clothes than you could wear in weeks, months, or years? As you were counting up your clothing did you notice that there were many pieces that you have not touched in ages—or possibly never worn at all? I'm not surprised. It all comes down to the 80/20 Rule: We wear 20 percent of our clothes 80 percent of the time. If you are like most people, you've probably never worn many of the clothes in your closet. Or you

THE REVERSE CLOTHES HANGER TRICK

Turn all of the clothes hanging in your closet so that the hangers face back-to-front. For the next six months, if you wear an item of clothing, return it to the closet with the hanger facing the correct way. No cheating. If you try it on but decide not to wear it, make sure you put it back with the hanger turned backwards. Be prepared for a shock when after six months you look at the clothes that are on hangers that are still reversed. These are the clothes you have not worn and you should seriously consider getting rid of them all.

have worn them so infrequently that you would not notice if they disappeared.

You may think there are only a few items that never see the light of day but here's foolproof way to really convince yourself about the clothes you do, and do not, wear. It's called the Reverse Clothes Hanger Trick.

If you are not wearing your clothes there are usually a couple of reasons:

1. They don't fit.

Look at your chart. What size are you now and what size are the clothes you have? How many of your clothes actually fit you today? Obviously, there are some exceptions—postpregnancy, for example—but the basic rule is clear: if it doesn't fit, it needs to go. I've seen plenty of closets filled with "wish" clothes that will be worn when someone wishes their way to a smaller waist, less weight, or whatever is keeping them from fitting into the clothes today. The problem with wish clothes is that we think they will serve as an incentive to fit into them but what they really do is to mock, making us feel guilty and inadequate. They become a constant reminder that we are not that particular size—who needs to be reminded of that perceived failure every time you go in the closet? Not only that, they use up valuable space in the closet that can be use for clothes that make you feel good about yourself. Dress for the body you have and the life you live now.

2. I spent good money on them

Whether they were a splurge or a steal, you've spent the money already and it's time to face the facts. It's not a bargain if you don't ever wear it. I don't care how much it was marked down, or what designer is on the label. If you don't wear it, it is money you've already spent and it continues to cost you every day in psychic and physical space. Give it away or sell it. The guilt of having spent money on something you don't wear shouldn't be the motivating factor for holding onto your clothes.

Touch and go

It is difficult to let go of things you have spent money on—sometimes a lot of money—but really, what is the point of clothing that doesn't suit you or flatter your figure? Dress for the life you want for yourself! Get rid of the clothing that doesn't match your vision and clear some space to see what you have. Give you and your clothes some room to breathe and you'll feel great when you go to your closet to choose what to wear. Enjoy the positive feedback and compliments from wearing clothes that suit you. Wear clothes that reflect the new uncluttered and organized you!

Look at the piles on your bed and look at the list you made. You now have to make decisions about what is going back in you closet. Go pile by pile and as you touch each item use the flow chart on page 84.

As you sort through the clothing in your closet, keep in mind your vision of where you want your life to be. Each item you put on the discard pile represents one step closer to that life.

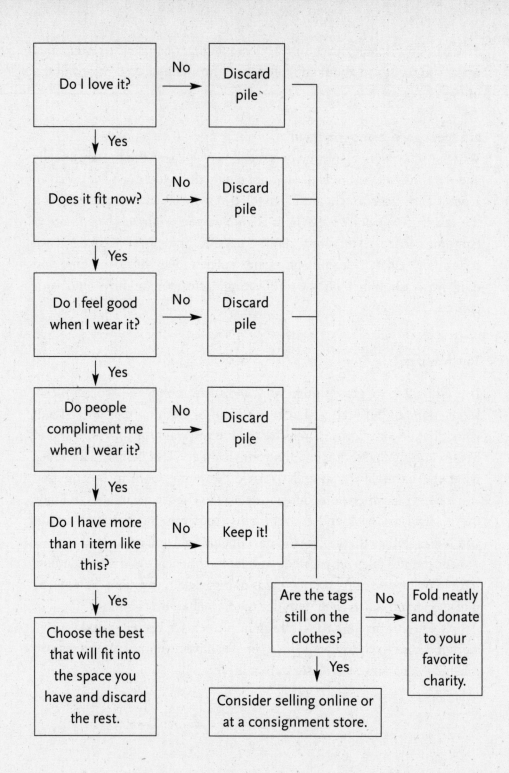

STORAGE

The majority of your closet should be filled with clothes you wear frequently and look and feel good in. Clothes are easier to find if you clean and store off-season items. Use the seasonal switch (see below) to get rid of the past season's clothes that you didn't end up wearing and do the same for the next season's clothes that don't look appealing when you pull them out of storage.

Troubleshooting in the closet

Make use of storage systems that allow you to keep your things neatly and clearly see what you have. Over-the-door shoe pockets, belt and tie racks and hangers, sweater boxes, and more can help keep you organized. Be sure that any boxes that you can't see through are clearly labeled with what's inside. Designate a shelf or box for a particular item—winter handbags go in the box in summer; the summer handbags go in the box in winter. If you maintain a rotating system you will always be able to find what you need and be able to assess when it is time to let it go.

Keep like things together by color and style

We tend to find a style we like and a color that looks good on us and buy the same thing over and over again. Having multiples of similar items tells me that you are unaware of what you've got. Arranging by color and style will allow you to really see what you've got.

Shoes

What is it about shoes? We've only got two feet but I've seen shoe "collections" that are big enough to cover the feet of every man, woman, and child in a small country. I've also seen shoes that have overrun the closet and are being stored in spare rooms, under beds, in attics, under desks at the office, and more. Just like clothes, shoes can be "wish" items. You see a pair on sale and buy them because they are such a great deal and you will look beautiful in them *next* season. Or they fit perfectly in the store, but they slip/pinch/scrape your heel when you get them home. Or you discover that they don't go with that dress you thought they would but they might go with something else you haven't bought yet. You probably held onto them because you paid good money for them and it feels like a waste to get rid of them. In reality, it's more of a waste to keep them around contributing to the clutter in your closet.

A compounding problem is that we tend to have shoes for very specific purposes—dress shoes, rain boots, running shoes, tennis shoes, slippers, gardening clogs. The way shoes are so specialized it's no wonder they become a storage and clutter problem. The first step (no pun intended) in getting a grip on your shoes—just as you did with your clothes—is to pull them out of your closet and sort them by type/color, and style. Make a list, giving a line to *each* pair of shoes, not just the kind of shoe. I know this seems crazy but it is really important. Shoes are emotional items and if you don't face each pair square on, you risk giving in and putting them back in the closet.

Other questions I want you to ask yourself with each pair: Why did I buy these? Who did I think I would be/become with these shoes? Why am I keeping them? When did I buy them? How many times have I worn them? Are they worth keeping?

On the following list, circle the pairs of shoes that you have worn in the last month. You can keep two pairs of each type of shoe and one pair of slippers or specialty shoes like gardening clogs. Easy there, if you don't have two pairs of sneakers this isn't license to go out and buy them!

Once you have determined what shoes you are going to keep (no duplicates, no shoes that don't fit, no shoes that are beyond repair, and no seasonal shoes you haven't worn in the last two months) you need to figure out how to store them so you can find what you need when you need it. Digging through a pile of shoes at the bottom of the closet just doesn't work. Commit to keeping your shoes neat and accessible. Sort them by

Shoes	How many?	Color(s)	Is there an outfit it goes with?
Sneaker	_____	_____	_____
Boots	_____	_____	_____
Loafers	_____	_____	_____
Dress shoes	_____	_____	_____
Flats	_____	_____	_____
Heels	_____	_____	_____
Sandals	_____	_____	_____
Flip flops	_____	_____	_____
Clogs	_____	_____	_____
Sling backs	_____	_____	_____
Slippers	_____	_____	_____
_____	_____	_____	_____
_____	_____	_____	_____
_____	_____	_____	_____

color and put them in a shoe rack (approximately eight inches per pair per foot of space), or put them in a hanging shoe bag that fits over the back of your closet door or in a hanging shoe bag that goes on the bar in the closet. If you keep shoes in boxes, be sure they are labeled clearly so you know what you have or they'll stay in boxes.

You just did a lot of work to clear out your closet. Congratulations. But let's be clear here: If you emptied out your shoes and you still have twenty-plus pairs, you have too many shoes and you need to do this again.

IF THE SHOE FITS

Once you have your shoes sorted out, put a slip of paper inside the shoe near the heel. If you wear the shoe take out and discard the paper. At the end of six months, see if any shoes have slips of paper left in them. If you haven't worn the shoes for seasonal reasons, fair enough, they can stay in your closet. If, however, the season was right but the shoe never got out into the world then it is time to say good-bye.

Finally, from now on, to avoid ending up in the same situation, when you buy a pair of shoes, you have to discard a pair of shoes. It's simple—one in, one out.

We often use closet space for more than clothes and shoes. If you must put other items in the closet be sure that you are doing so consciously and choosing to keep them—not just shoving something in the closet because there is nowhere else for it to go.

HANDBAGS

Handbags, like shoes tend to multiply in the dark. You must pare down your collection to fit the space you have. Give your bags a once-over. Do the zippers work? Is the lining torn? Is there a stain that you can't get out? Is the handle hanging on by a thread? Get rid of any bags you haven't used in the last year. Then, sort your handbags by color and season. As with your shoes, put a slip of paper inside each handbag. If at the end of six months a bag still has its slip of paper, the handbag needs to go.

Off-season clothing

No one wants to have to dig past wooly turtlenecks to unearth that short-sleeved shirt that is more appropriate for the summer weather. Depending on the size of your closet, you can have cool weather clothes on one side and warmer weather clothes on the other. Perhaps you can have a hanging rack in the front and one in the back and rotate your clothes seasonally. If space is tight, it is extremely helpful to have a designated spot for your off-season garb. A trunk at the end of the bed or one that serves as a bedside table that can also be used for out-of-season clothes is a great solution. Keeping your clothes sorted by season allows you complete access to your clothes and switching from one season to another provides a great opportunity to determine which clothes are working for you and which need to go.

The seasonal switch

You'll need three bags—one for repair/clean, one for thrift store/sell, one for trash

1. Pick a day and time.
2. Get your stored clothes out and put them on your bed sorted by category (shirts, sweaters, pants, etc.).
3. Open your closets and drawers.
4. Take out the seasonal clothes you are about to store and try on each item. Then, depending on how it fits, either put it in one of the designated bags or move it to the storage space that has been vacated by the incoming clothing. Remember, if it doesn't fit or if you haven't worn it in the last six months—it goes!
5. When you are ready to put away the new season's clothes you also must sort them into the appropriate bags or place them in your closet or drawers.

6. Toss the clothes that are too worn or damaged to donate. Put the clothes that need cleaning and repair by the front door so you can take them to the cleaners/tailors immediately. Put the (folded and neatly sorted) clothes you are donating into a bag and on your next trip out the door take it to a charity or to your local thrift shop. See Resources for information on charitable giving.

7. Take all the wire hangers that seem to have been breeding in your closet and recycle them at your drycleaners.

The dresser/bureau/chest of drawers

This handy item is known by many names and usually holds things like socks, underwear, shirts, accessories, and anything that can be folded up and put in a drawer. Drawers very often become a case of out of sight, out of mind, so you are going to empty your drawers to clear the clutter and make it easier to find the clothes that fit and that you love to wear. When your bureau is empty, take the opportunity to clean the drawers, line them with drawer liners, and move the bureau away from the wall and clean behind it. Wow! Is that the earring you lost two years ago?

The questions that need to be answered with this piece of bedroom furniture are, *What's on it?* and *What's in it?*

The top of a dresser can become a repository for makeup, hairbrushes, loose change, ticket stubs, keys, eyeglasses, and more. Write down all of the things that are on your dresser/bureau top. Are there hair products, hand or body lotions, make-up, hair brush, comb, mirror, jewelry, buttons, hair elastics, hair clips, CDs, DVDs, tweezers, watch, pencils, pens, cell phone, loose change, mail, bills, books, magazines, nail file, "decorative" items like boxes or bowls, photographs, and more? Be specific.

What's on it?   **Why is it there?**

_____   _____

_____   _____

Now, think about how you want to use the top of your dresser and how it fits into your vision of your bedroom. Write here what you will keep on your dresser that serves your vision of how the dresser fulfills its function in your bedroom.

_____

_____

_____

Take five minutes and purge the top of your dresser of the things that don't belong. You have four kinds of things on your dresser:

1. Items that belong elsewhere.
2. Items that belong to someone else.
3. Things that should be thrown away.
4. Things that belong there.

What's in my drawers? (drawer by drawer)

Here too, be as specific as possible. Don't write "shirts"—say how many and what color they are.

Drawer 1: _____

_____

Drawer 2: _____

_____

Drawer 3: _____

_____

Drawer 4: _____

_____

Now, let's take a look inside at just some of the typical contents of a dresser and the clutter problems they can create.

Socks. Socks have a way of disappearing—usually every time you do laundry. I don't know where the orphaned socks go but it's a safe bet that you will never see the missing socks again.

1. Empty your sock drawer onto your bed.
2. Discard any single socks, any that are torn or that are soiled.
3. Fold pairs together and only return to the drawer the number that will reasonably fit. You only have two feet and there are only seven days in a week. Nobody needs a drawer overflowing with socks.
4. Do the same for hose, tights, and stockings.

Underwear. Just because it is out of sight doesn't mean it should be unsightly!

1. Take out all your underwear, bras, slips, camisoles, etc. and put them on the bed.
2. Get rid of any underwear that is clearly past its use-by date. Spare me the details. Just do it.
3. Don't keep bras that don't fit just because they were expensive.
4. Get rid of slips, camisoles, and other undergarments that you never wear or that don't fit.
5. Return the undergarments to the drawer neatly and sorted by type.

T-shirts. One of the main offenders of clothing clutter are T-shirts. Souvenirs, give-aways, and sporting events contribute to an awful lot of cotton shirts filling up valuable clothing space. Gather up all of your T-shirts and put them on your bed.

1. Discard anything with holes or stains.
2. Make piles sorted by color.

3. Cut back the number to reasonably fit into their assigned space by getting rid of one for every three or four you keep until you are at the right number.
4. Return them to the drawer, sorted by color, so you can always find what you need.
5. Repeat the T-shirt exercise with any other shirts you keep in your drawers—turtlenecks, polo shirts, button-downs, etc.

Consider using drawer dividers (particularly with socks, hose, bras, underwear) to establish zones within your drawers for those items. Remember if it is always in the same place and with other things like it you can always find what you need.

Accessories. Accessories are the small extra additions—a scarf, a necklace, cufflinks—that make a good outfit great. Remember that with accessories a little goes a long way.

Jewelry may seem so small that it can't possibly cause clutter. But jewelry is very hard to store neatly and most people only wear a fraction of what they have. I want you to enjoy what you have to the fullest through organization, even when it comes to the smallest details.

All that glitters

Here is how to get a handle on your jewelry, wear and enjoy what you most value, and let go of the things you no longer want.

1. Invest in a jewelry box that has space for earrings, necklaces, bracelets, and rings. This jewelry box will be the place for your jewelry. When it's full—that's it. No more unless something else goes.
2. Throw away all the little boxes the jewelry came in and put the jewelry in your jewelry box. You won't need those boxes in the future. If you buy someone a gift of jewelry, it will come in its own box.

3. Get rid of everything you don't wear. If you've been holding onto something because you think it might be valuable, then get to eBay and find out what it might be worth. If it no longer matches your style or is outdated, let it go.

4. If you've inherited something and feel you must keep it, ask yourself why? Is having it a burden rather than a gift? If you want to honor the memory but not wear the jewelry, can you create a shadow box with the jewelry and a photo of the person who left it to you? But before you do this, be honest: Do you have somewhere to hang that shadowbox? If not, this is just a suggestion and not a solution.

5. Do you have something so valuable that you are afraid to wear it? Talk to your insurance agent and have it added to your homeowner's policy. Or put it in a safe deposit box but definitely get it out for special occasions.

6. If you have something like costume jewelry that isn't worth selling, but you don't wear, consider giving it to someone (child, family member, or a friend) who will wear it and enjoy it. Otherwise get rid of it.

7. Get rid of anything that is broken or get it repaired. If an earring is missing its mate—toss it. Much like socks, the missing earring rarely turns up. One way to stop this from happening, if your jewelry box doesn't have a special place for earrings, is to try pinning pierced earrings through a piece of fabric as soon as you take them off and putting the fabric into your jewelry box. This prevents them from getting lost or separated. Use a ring holder to keep rings stacked, visible, and ready to wear.

8. Make your jewelry as accessible as possible And use what you've got. You didn't buy those dazzling earrings so they can sit in a dark box. Get them out and put them on. I'm not suggesting wearing your best jewels to the gym, but go ahead and wear what you've got and love. And if you still find yourself wearing the same things over and over again remember that the next time you are enticed by the jewelry counter at the mall, walk past it. You have enough!

Bedside table

A bedside table is often the bedroom version of the kitchen junk drawer. It becomes a place where odds and ends accumulate to the point where it's a clutter container and not a useful piece of bedroom furniture. Take a look at your bedside table and list everything that is on it, under it, and stuffed inside it. Are books and magazines stacked so high you can't read the time on your clock? Are the things on the bedside table yours, or have the kids taken over that space as well? Again, be as specific as possible when you list what is here.

What's on it?

_____

_____

_____

Why is that stuff there?

_____

_____

_____

What's in it?

_____

_____

Why is that stuff there?

_____

_____

Now ask yourself if the items that are on and in your bedside table are contributing to the vision you have for your master bedroom. Take five minutes and get rid of the bits of papers, reshelve the books, and recycle those ancient magazines. Now maybe you can actually see your alarm clock and have space for the book you are currently reading.

RELAXING

If you have space in your bedroom for a corner where you can read, listen to music, meditate, or simply unwind and relax you want to be sure that you have the things you need to do so. A comfy chair, a good light, and a place for your music will help make your bedroom a refuge and a place where you can recharge. But before we start this, be completely honest— if your room is too small for this function *do not* clutter it with more furniture. Sometimes a bedroom can just be a *bed*room.

My relaxation zone

It is very important to create sanctuary spaces in your home (every family member needs one). What is your vision for this space? What did you include on your vision board? List the things you will need to create an oasis of calm where you can do what you need to recharge your batteries. If you share this room don't forget to include your partner's vision too.

Furniture _____

Lighting _____

Audio _____

Tools for activity (books, knitting, Sudoku puzzles, pencil) _____

_____

_____

Beware, however, because you can really defeat the purpose of the relaxation zone if it becomes a place where you toss dirty or rejected items of clothing. Remember that if you take something off, hang it up or put it in the hamper. If you decide not to wear something because it's not right for the event, by all means, return it to the closet. If, however, you decide not to wear it because it doesn't look good, you don't like it anymore, or if it doesn't fit, move it straightaway to your charity bag.

Also, don't let a hobby take over the room. If you do needlepoint while sitting in that cozy corner, don't let your canvases and threads creep over to the bureau or your bed.

Tools for the bedroom

A waste paper basket. If you don't have a place to put papers, tissues, and such they will inevitably end up on any horizontal surface that they can find. Use a waste paper basket and empty it on a regular basis (at least once a week).

A hamper. Clean clothes get put away in the closet or drawers. Dirty clothes live in a hamper before their trip to the laundry or drycleaners. Clothes, dirty or otherwise, do not belong on the floor!

A charity bag. This is a bag that can be kept in your closet. When the kids outgrow their clothes, toss them in here (the clothes, not the kids!). When you put on something that doesn't fit, doesn't look good, or doesn't make you feel good when you wear it, toss it in here. When the bag is full, it's time to take it off to your favorite local charity. (But make sure they are laundered, sorted, and folded neatly.)

You have done a huge job! Look around your new clean room. Doesn't it feel great to see your clean bedroom closet and dresser drawers and not only know what you have but know that you love what you have? You now truly have room to dress, sleep, and relax!

REALITY CHECK—GIVING TO CHARITIES

Goodwill receives a billion pounds of clothing every year. Ultimately, they use less than half of the clothing they get. Clothing is cheap. The cost of sorting, cleaning, storing, and transporting the clothes is often higher than their value. If you wouldn't give an article to a family member, it's probably not good enough for charity. Sure, it's great to get the tax deduction and it makes you feel like you didn't waste money buying the clothes, but if you're truly charitable, be sensitive to the needs of the organization. Charities aren't dumping grounds for your trash. Talk to your local charities or visit CharityNavigator.org. Find out what they can most use. Although giving to charities is a great way to get stuff out of your house, it's far better not to let stuff into your house in the first place. (See the Resources section for organizations that will take your gently used clothing.)

———

Now that the master bedroom is clean and clutter free, write down how it feels.

_____

_____

Make the commitment, right here and now to keep it looking as it does at this moment.

I will commit to taking care of this room by doing the following:

Daily: Make bed, clothes in hamper, if something is taken out, it is put away, five-minute purge

Weekly: Empty waste paper basket, dust, vacuum, wash bed linens, take care of laundry and dry cleaning, shelve books, recycle magazines, clear dresser top and bedside tables

Monthly: Assess what clothes and shoes haven't been worn.

Every six months: Seasonal clothes swap and purge, clean up and organize drawers and closet

Yearly: Stand outside the room and reassess its ideal function. Is it still achieving its ideal function? What's getting in the way?

5

Kids' Rooms

WHETHER IT'S DUE to a zoo of stuffed animals, schoolbooks and sporting equipment, or the classic unmade bed, kids' rooms can be some of the most cluttered rooms in the house. Sure, kids can be messy but you don't have to look far to see the immediate influence that contributes to kid clutter. Yep, Mom and Dad, I'm looking at you. Kids will follow your lead so it's up to you to teach them, and show them, how to maintain their rooms and their things with the respect those things deserve.

THINK IT THROUGH

Kids have more access than ever to vast amounts of information and a great deal of media influence and advertising. More than ever it is imperative for parents to be parents, to demonstrate by their words and actions what they value, and to model the behavior they desire for their kids. In my experience, the less clutter and more organization you can build into your home, the less stress, more fun, and greater harmony you'll enjoy.

SET IT UP

Now, let's take a minute and pull together all the hard work and thought you and your child[ren] have put into envisioning the ideal room. Pull out your vision board and your lists to use for the work you are about to do to get this room in shape.

Goals (from page 32): _____

Ideal function (from page 45): _____

What has to go (from page 56): _____

_____

What it should contain (from page 57): _____

_____

MAKE IT HAPPEN

Of all the rooms in your house the kids' rooms are the ones that change the most over time to accommodate their growing up and changing interests. Sometimes it's harder for parents to let go of childhood things and let the vision of a room change and grow than it is for your child. Keep that in mind while you do this cleanup. The room may be in your house but it is your child's room. Respect his or her ideas and input and you will have a room that works for both of you.

Stand outside of your child's room with your child. Both of you can answer these questions:

- What do you see?

_____

- What was your vision of this room when you moved to the house?

_____

- What does it look like now?

_____

- What is this room's function now?

_____

- What is the function you want it to have? Do you and your child share this view?

_____

_____

- In order to serve its function, what furniture, contents, and open space should the room contain?

Furniture: _____

Contents: _____

Open space: _____

- What is on the floor? Wall-to-wall? Area rugs? Can you see the floor?

_____

- What is on the walls? Photos? Paintings? Nothing? (Are things still waiting to be hung?)

_____

- When was the last time this room was painted?

_____

- Does each item in this room enhance and fulfill the purpose for this room?

_____

- If you didn't know, could you tell what age child used this room?

_____

- Is there space for your child to sleep, play, daydream, do homework?

_____

- Are there places for clothes, books, toys that are easily accessible for your child?

_____

- Does this room look like your ideal of a child's room or does it reflect your child's ideal?

_____

- Ask your child what he or she would like the room to be like. Write it down here. You may discover something new about your child, her interests, and her sense of style.

_____

_____

_____

AS THEY GROW

Kids' needs in a home and the way they use a room can change dramatically over time.

Infants/toddlers/preschoolers

You will largely be making the decisions about what will go in your baby's or small child's room. Don't ask: What will fit in here? Ask: What can I put in this room to create the safe, warm, and quiet haven for my child? As kids grow they can be taught to put things back where they got them. In fact, at the end of every play session, help your child to put his toys back on shelves or in the toy box—it's a good habit that can't be started early enough.

Elementary school aged kids

Obviously there is a huge range in interests and activities from kindergarten through middle school but children in these years can learn to take care of their things, value what they have, and make choices about how they play and use their space in their rooms. Don't wait until they are asleep to sort through art or school work or toys—have them do it with you. Involve them in packing up outgrown clothes for charity, discarding old stuffed animals, and give them some choices about what will be in their room. Allow them to express their wishes and make choices. Keep it simple by asking them to choose, say, between two colors for the bedding rather than opening it up to multiple choices. Make them a part of any cleanup process so they can learn what to do, how to make those choices, and develop good habits for the future.

Teens

Suffice it to say that teens are usually searching for their own style and sense of space. Don't be surprised if your teen doesn't want you in his or her room. However, it's up to you to insist on and enforce basic cleanliness and be sure that clothes, sheets, and towels are getting in the laundry, etc. In any family discussion, teens can bring a fresh perspective to ideas on how to use common rooms. Don't reject their input out of hand—you may hear a great idea that can change your home for the better!

MAPPING THE ZONES

When you establish the zones with your child, it's important to help him or her understand where things belong in the room and in the house by creating clear areas for like items. This reinforces the concept of everything having a proper place and makes it easier for children to tidy the room. It helps them take responsibility for order in their space.

Kid's bedroom zones
- Sleeping
- Clothes

- Shoes
- Homework
- Toys
- Reading
- Arts and Crafts
- Music

The kids' rooms got a quick purge at the start of this process. Now take a minute with your child to review how to do a quick five minute clean-up so she will establish the habit. For the cleanup you are about to do set aside an hour or two hours (with the kids you may have to break this time into smaller increments to keep their attention and get their assistance).

SLEEPING

A school-aged child should be making his or her own bed, every day. I wouldn't worry about enforcing hospital corners but the bed should at least look like someone tried to straighten it up.

Bed check

We asked questions like this about the master bedroom, and they are as important for your kids' comfort and growth as they are for you.

Are the mattress and box spring comfortable and age appropriate?

_____

Is it time to replace them?

_____

Are the sheets clean?

_____

Is the bedspread/duvet/blanket without stains or tears?

_____

Is the bed covering cleaned regularly?

_____

Are the pillows comfortable? Have they lost their shape and support?

_____

_____

Is the bed overrun with stuffed animals that need to be removed every night to make room for sleep? (More on stuffed animals later.)

_____

_____

Just as in the master bedroom there should be nothing under the bed. Kids are kids and things will find their way under there but it shouldn't be a permanent home for anything. Any clutter purge should start with an exploration under the bed.

CLOTHES

With kids, clothing management is more a function of keeping on top of what they have grown out of or worn out and not the volume problem encountered in most adults' closets. However, don't let your kid's closet become an extension of your bad shopping habits—she doesn't "need" four navy blue sweaters anymore than you do, no matter how cute or what a bargain they are.

What kids really need is a place where their clothes can be kept neatly. One of the challenges for kids is that they can't reach adult-size shelves, hooks, or drawers. If your child can't reach to put things away designate a reachable spot for his clothes. A kid-sized clothes rack is a great place for hanging dirty clothes and for putting out the next day's outfit. Be sure there is a designated spot for shoes and slippers. Boots

WHERE IS MY . . . ?

A great way to keep kids' things organized is to have a bag on a hook or a basket near the front door (or whichever door you most use to leave the house). Backpacks can be left there, along with homework folders (once homework is completed); in winter that's where hats, scarves, and gloves will go. In summer, hats, sunglasses, and sunscreen can be held there. Rather than everyone scrambling in the morning to collect these items from all over the house, they will be right there, waiting to go.

To keep track of kids' things when they are out in the world, put sew-in, iron-on, or adhesive name tape in clothing they are likely to leave behind—coats, scarves, mittens, etc. They can even be used in shoes and boots.

Mom and dad can use a system like this for keys, sun or eyeglasses, briefcases or shoulder bags and backpacks.

Because kids grow so quickly, it is really important to do the seasonal switch with their clothes to assess what does and doesn't fit. What might have looked great in May can be ragged and too short by September. Or you could have a sundress at the end of the summer with the tags still on it that she never wore. It can be very painful—after all, you spent good money on it—but if it doesn't fit or she is never going to wear it, it has to go. And if it fits now but it won't next year, it has to go. Kids grow fast. Their tastes change. Don't hold onto something because you love it even if your son doesn't or because it reminds you of when he was at his cutest. He will be cute again and if you give that beautiful shirt to someone who needs it and can use it now you are doing something good for someone else and for yourself. And you are teaching your child two good lessons about letting go and sharing.

and outerwear may be in a closet in another part of the house, but be sure kids know where they belong. These items should be returned there after use and not plopped down in the middle of the bedroom.

Kids also need to learn to care for their clothes and this they learn from you. Give them a hamper for dirty clothes that's easy to reach. Let them know that if clothes don't make it into the hamper, they don't make it into the laundry and they may just run out of things to wear!

Speaking of drawers. Do for your kid's clothes what you did for yours. Do a drawer by drawer search and purge of solo socks, soiled T-shirts, pants and tights with no knees, and anything that doesn't fit your child—or comfortably fit in the drawer space.

Drawer by drawer

Here too, be as specific as possible. Don't write "shirts"—say how many and what color they are and what size they are. And be honest. Are you still holding onto that size 3 T-shirt even though your daughter is now nine? You need to separate the sentimentality from the substance if you want to make this purge work.

Drawer 1: _____

_____

Drawer 2: _____

_____

Drawer 3: _____

_____

Drawer 4: _____

_____

Now, let's take a look inside at just some of the typical contents of a dresser and the clutter problems they can create.

Socks

Kids' socks and underwear have a way of multiplying, probably because as they grow you tend to add to your collection rather than replace the old with the new. I knew a mother whose eight-year-old daughters still had their size 4 underwear because it was still "good." It didn't fit and the girls never wore it because they also had size 5, 6, 7, and 8 in the drawer too, but she never threw the old ones away.

1. Empty the sock drawer onto the bed. Go through your laundry basket and hamper and get all those socks too, even if they are dirty, and dump them on the bed.
2. Discard any single socks and any that are torn or soiled. And check the size. Kids' feet grow as fast as the rest of them and a tight

sock is uncomfortable. Discard any socks that are not your child's size.

3. Fold pairs together and only return to the drawer the number that will reasonably fit. Nobody needs a drawer overflowing with socks.

Underwear. Just because it is out of sight doesn't mean it should be unsightly!

1. Get rid of any underwear that is clearly past its use-by date. Spare me the details. Just do it.

T-shirts. School, camp, sports teams, vacation souvenirs all seem to have designated T-shirts that can fill up a drawer faster than anything else.

1. Pull all the T-shirts out of the drawer.
2. Immediately discard anything that is worn, torn, or stained.
3. Immediately discard anything that is not your child's current size or the next size he or she will grow into—determine if it is in good enough shape to pass on to a friend, a younger family member, or a charity and do so immediately.
4. Go through the T-shirts with the goal of cutting the number until they fit reasonably into their alloted space.

Repeat the T-shirt exercise with other tops, skirts, dresses, pants, pajamas, sweatpants, sweatshirts, and sweaters.

As I hope you're starting to realize by now the only answer to managing inflow is to create an equal volume of outflow. The same rules that apply to your clothes apply to your kids' clothes: You can only keep what you wear.

Where should the old clothes go?

1. Anything stained or beyond repair should go in the trash or somewhere like an animal shelter that uses old clothing as rags.
2. Find a friend or a charity to bring a load of outgrown hand-me-downs to every six months.
3. Talk with other parents in your child's playgroup or preschool— look for creative ways to pass hand-me-downs to others who will value and use them. You'll make some lucky kid very happy and save some parent's budget serious strain!
4. There are organizations that take gently used children's clothing; see the Resources section for information on where to donate gently used clothing.

SHOES

Shoes are something kids often grow out of before they wear them out so it's worthwhile to pay close attention to how shoes fit. Also, especially with younger kids, it is unlikely that shoes will last more than a season so at the end of winter, throw away or give away those snow boots. That way, you won't be thinking you have boots for your child only to discover, on the morning of the giant snowstorm, that they don't fit.

Kid's do not need a lot of shoes. One pair of school shoes, sneakers, snow boots (if you live in a state that has snow), dress shoes (if they are going to wear them), sandals, and specific sports shoes. If your child has more shoes than that you really need to figure out why. Considering how quickly they grow out of them, buying more than the necessary shoes for your kids really is throwing money away.

Hanging shoe organizers with pockets are a great way for kids to be able to find and put away their shoes. A shoe organizer can be hung inside the closet door or anywhere that is within your child's reach.

SPORTS EQUIPMENT

If you have the room it is better to keep sports equipment all in one place in the house. The mudroom, garage, or basement are preferable. Plastic crates or tubs labeled with each family member's name is a good way to help keep everything sorted and easy to find. Keeping that crate by the front door is also a good way to keep the dirt from being tracked all through the house.

Things like cleats, ice skates, and other sports equipment are often grown out of before they wear out. If there are younger children in the league, team, or sports program make a connection with the parent of a child who could use the hand-me-down items and who might have the next size you are looking for. Swapping items like this is a great way to save some money and conserve some resources too. Or get a few parents together and sell all the outgrown items at the ice rink or baseball field. The money you raise can go toward fundraising for the team or a pizza party for the end of the season.

HOMEWORK

School-aged children need a clean, well-lighted place to do their homework. Ideally this is a desk in their room but it can be anywhere that is quiet so they can concentrate, and out of the way of the household bustle so they won't be interrupted. The desk should also have room for school supplies and there should be a waste basket for discarded papers. This space can double as an area to do crafts or hobbies, as long as crafting tools and school supplies are clearly kept separated in drawers or storage bins.

The desk is an area that can accumulate lots of papers, books, and sometimes clothing, toys, or electronics. At the end of every week do a Five-Minute Purge to toss the scrap paper and put non-desk items back where they belong.

As part of the Five-Minute Purge, test papers and worksheets that have been handed in and marked can be put in a folder in a drawer of the desk. At the end of the school year save only the papers that are truly a cut above the rest—the A+ report, the kindergartener's first story, the 100% on a tough math test—and toss the rest.

TOYS

A common problem I encounter in homes with children is that the kids' rooms are overwhelmed with toys. And guess what? The kids can be pretty overwhelmed too. With so many options they halfheartedly play with one toy, grab another, pull out a game, and become "bored" quickly. Unfortunately, the typical parental solution is to get something new, further adding to the chaos and clutter. The real solution is to limit the amount of toys, books, and games.

Once the number of toys is reduced, they can be stored in bins, hanging shoe containers, or toy hammocks and once full, no more toys come in.

Toys with small parts can be kept in open-ended containers or baskets on a low shelf in a bookcase. Again, like items go with like items. All toy cars go in one bin, same for model horses or whatever your child has multiples of.

One In, One Out

One way to keep a lid on an excess of toys is to establish the One In, One Out Rule. If something new comes into the house, something old needs to go to make space for it. And it has to be something of equal size. No trading a toy car for a huge doll house. I know this can be tough rule to keep, especially at birthdays and holidays, but it is possible. Every trip to the zoo or museum doesn't have to end with a trip to the gift shop but if it does, then something will have to go before the new toy or game enters the house. Make sure your children know and understand this rule. Every time you are shopping and they want a new toy, ask them what they are going to let go of to make room. By giving them the choice you are letting them decide what they want and what they want to keep. It also stops the "I want that" tantrums. Kids learn that things have a real cost—and it makes them more responsible with what they own.

The toy store in the closet

There is a way to divide and conquer when it comes to toys. You can remove a number of games or toys from your kid's room or playroom and keep them in a box in the closet. When he says he has nothing to play with, tell him to grab something he's tired of and exchange it for something from the "Toy Store in the Closet." When children, especially younger ones, haven't seen a toy in some time, they will think of it as something new. You will have pared down the number of toys in your child's room and found an inexpensive way to bring a new toy into your child's playtime. If they are uninterested in the "new" toys, it is time to sell or give them away.

Hibernation

A variation on the toy store in the closet is "hibernation." Your child chooses a few stuffed animals or toys to go into "hibernation," which is a bag or box in the closet. At the end of three months, if he or she has not requested that a toy come out of hibernation, then that toy is given away or discarded.

Toy exchange

Arrange to swap toys with a friend or neighbor. Or reach out through the Internet to sites like Freecycle or Toyswap.com (where you can sell or swap toys) to get the old toys out of the house. Involve your child in these decisions—ask which toy she'd like to swap and see if you can find something she'd like in exchange. Consider donating toys to charity, school, or a shelter. This does not work with stuffed animals, which no organizations accept because of germs. That's another good reason to keep a limit on how many you bring home.

By teaching your child to manage toys well you will teach your child so much more than how to play. Children need the basics to survive and thrive—love, food, and shelter. Without these necessities life would be impossible. But they also need two other basics—limits and routines. Kids thrive on limits and relish routines. Create a life model by setting and enforcing reasonable limits and establishing clear routines.

Toy limits

It's tempting to give kids a constant supply of new toys to keep them occupied. Of course it's easier to fulfill their requests (or demands!) for new entertainment than to plan a play date or find time to go to a museum or park.

LESSONS LEARNED FROM TOY LIMITS

Setting limits teaches the child:

- You can't own everything.
- There is joy and satisfaction in giving to others who are less fortunate.
- Mom and Dad (or the grandparents) are not a bottomless pit of supply.
- You must make decisions surrounding the things you own.
- You must decide what is important to you, value it, and look after it.

Provide your child with a couple of bins for toys—two or three—whatever is reasonable for the space you have. These bins are where the toys live. Not on the furniture in the family room, or in mom and dad's room, or in the back seat of the car. Cloth hanging shoe organizers can be a great way to store small stuffed animals or toys. There are a finite number of pockets and a finite number of cuddly toys that can fit in this "wall zoo." If one goes in, one has to come out to make room.

This may seem harsh, but children do not need an endless supply of things to be happy. And it is a parent's obligation to help the child create a world in which solid values come before the acquisition of the latest video game or newest gadget. This investment when the child is young will yield huge dividends later on in life.

Outgrown toys

Kids outgrow everything quickly, including their interest in toys. It's important to regularly sort toys *with your kids* to discard and pass on everything that they have outgrown, that they no longer play with, or that is damaged. Don't do this on your own. Involve the kids in deciding what should stay and what should go. If you do it without them they will resent you for it and feel a loss for things that they may no longer really care about anyway. You can do a quick purge every two or three months. Just grab a box or bin and head with your kids to their play area. Go through the bins and baskets and shelves and pull out anything you think should go. You'll be surprised how many broken bits have accumulated in those bins. Your kids will tell you what they want to keep and what they think should go. It only takes twenty minutes and it is worth it. And it helps prepare them for the larger purge you will do twice a year.

The seasonal purge

Inevitably there are toys that never get played with, books that are no longer of interest, or things that your kids have outgrown.

REALITY CHECK—GRANDPARENTS AND TOYS

When grandparents visit they often want to achieve the Santa Claus effect. They come loaded with toys in hopes of spoiling and delighting their beloved grandchildren. It's tough to say no, but here are some suggestions you can give them for more practical gift giving.

- Set up a college fund to which they can contribute.
- Set up a travel fund that, when your child turns sixteen, will pay for her to take a trip with her grandparents.
- Suggest specific toys that you would have bought your child anyway—toys that serve a real function in the child's development.
- Suggest ways they can show their love through *experiences* instead of stuff. Remind them that sharing an experience with her grandparents is as exciting to your daughter as receiving stuff. She won't remember her Elmo doll for long, but if she learns to appreciate new experiences they'll be helping to create a pattern that will last the child's whole life.
- Take the kids to a show. Introduce them to musicals, ballet, or live theatre.
- Ask them to bring ingredients for a favorite family recipe and invite the child to help prepare it.

1. Schedule a time a week or two before birthdays or gift-receiving holidays and before school lets out for summer so that you and your child can go through his room and playroom to root out the things he no longer wants or needs.
2. Arrange the toys in distinct piles—either by type of toy, by age appropriateness, or by length of time the child has had the toy. This will help your children see the toys as distinct groups and make the task more manageable.

3. Agree on the volume of toys that is reasonable to keep, factoring in the size of the space, and work together to that goal.
4. Books or working toys or games can be given to charity or sold.
5. Game discs and cartridges can often be traded in for a credit toward a new game at the game store.

Why not inspire the entrepreneur in your children and let them have a mini-tag sale instead of a lemonade stand?

Toy routines

Just as limits are important in helping kids manage clutter, so are simple routines. In addition to owning a reasonable, manageable quantity of toys, children need to learn the regular rhythm of picking up after themselves. At the end of the play session or at the end of the day the toys need to be returned to their bins. If this seems unreasonable, go back to the vision you have for the life you want. If you want a lifetime of picking up after your children, this is where it starts. Your choice!

LESSONS LEARNED FROM TOY ROUTINES

This daily activity of returning toys to their homes teaches the child:

- The importance of personal responsibility.
- The fundamentals of being organized.
- The concepts of timetables and scheduling.
- To participate as a member of a larger family.
- To help with simple chores that grow as the child matures.

INTRODUCING YOUR CHILD TO GIVING

If letting go of once prized possessions is new and hard for your child, try the following techniques.

Meet the charity. Put a face to the recipient of your child's toys. Before giving anything away, go to a shelter or charity and show the child how his hand-me-downs will be used by someone who needs them more.

Demonstrate by example. Before asking your children to donate, involve them in your own donation project. Let them help you find clothes you never wear. Show them how happy you are about finding a "good home" for things you once loved. Ask them if they'd like to give it a try.

Situational education. When certain catastrophes, large and small, happen in the world and in your life, seize the moment to teach your child about giving. For example, a TV interview with a hurricane victim is a way to give a face to the clothes you're sending away. Or passing a homeless person on the street is a chance to explain that some people have a harder life, and we can help them.

Birthday giving. A child's birthday is a great time to pair the influx of gifts with some giving. Duplicate presents are easy to give away and help get the child used to the idea. It's also a good time to have a purge ritual for toys and clothes: "Now that you're such a big girl, let's see what you've outgrown."

Ask your child how it feels to clean out old toys and send them off to someone who will play with them and appreciate them. Write it down here:

_____

_____

_____

READING, CRAFTS, MUSIC

If your child wants to do crafts, or read or play music, she needs to have a designated space to do so. Otherwise it is an invitation for one activity to overwhelm the room, depriving her of a space to play freely.

Ask your child what she likes to do most and how she'd like to use the space in her room. If all she wants to do is collapse on a beanbag chair and read, then there isn't much point in creating a crafts' corner. A box of crafts items in a drawer of her desk may suffice if she only wants to do crafts occasionally.

Consider how the furniture in the room could be rearranged to accommodate her interests and activities. Be sure you have a designated spot and storage for each activity. A bookshelf for reading materials, a low shelf to store games, bins for toys, a table for painting or craft activities, a music stand and storage bins for sheet music, and so on. Ensure that the shelving and storage units are at the right height for the child and consistently reinforce the correct place for storing and displaying your child's belongings. If everything has a place to go, it is more likely that your child can clean up and put away items.

Refer to the Math of Stuff (page 64) to determine how much will fit in your designated spaces. Bins must contain the toys, not be overwhelmed by them.

ART AND SCHOOLWORK—TO KEEP OR NOT TO KEEP?

While it makes sense to keep some of the best pieces of your child's work, is it possible that the stuff you are keeping either represents something you yourself miss and yearn for or that you cannot separate the memory of your child's achievement from the piece itself? Both of these possibilities have some legitimacy, within reason. But it doesn't matter if it's for you or for your child. One thing is certain—you cannot and should not keep everything!

Ask yourself, "Why do I want to keep this particular piece of art?"

_____

_____

Ask your child, "Why do you want to keep this particular piece of art?"

_____

_____

You can't keep everything. Help your child sort through and pick the best painting, the best drawing. Make it a game, tell him you are playing Museum. The new museum (named after him, of course) can only have a certain number of pieces of art and he has to chose from his collection for it. He should come to realize that not all of his work is "museum-worthy" and learn an important lesson about placing relative value on his work.

Art archive

While it is tempting to keep everything and it seems heartless to throw out something your child has spent time creating, all pieces are not created equal. And, if they are piled high and spilling over surfaces they are not being seen and valued anyway. What to do? How do you pick and choose? And how do you break it to your child that a portion of the work you "oohed" and "aahed" over should be thrown away?

Tools for the art archive
- A flat portfolio
- Storage container
- Shelves
- Frames

Make selecting art that is worth keeping into a ceremony, not a purge.

1. File flat art in a portfolio.
2. At the end of each semester, tell your child it's time to pick the best of the best.
3. Go through the art and pick one piece to frame and three or four to keep for posterity.
4. The rest can be photographed and discarded. With digital photography and a digital frame you can create a rotating gallery of your child's art in a minimal space.
5. Use frames that allow you to easily swap in a new masterpiece from your prodigy to replace an old one. This strategy enables you to keep art pieces that your child values and loves. It also gives your child practice in discerning what to keep and what to let go—a valuable lesson for life and a real stumbling block for many people who struggle with clutter.

Three-dimensional art is trickier. What to do with the mock volcanoes and amorphous clay paperweights? Again, let them linger for a while, until the thrill has worn off, then decide whether something is for display or whether it was "a learning experience." If you or your child really wants to hold onto the piece, make sure that it is displayed well in a way that protects it from dust and damage.

SCHOOLWORK

By now you should have the hang of this! As with art, you must set a limit. Who are you keeping the schoolwork for—you, or your child? Designate a drawer, a folio, or a bin for the work you are going to keep. The size of this container sets the limit for how much you can save. Once the drawer is full, a piece has to be discarded before anything new can be added. One in, one out—it's a simple but effective strategy. At the end of each semester go through the drawer and assess what you have. I bet that English test is not as important now that he has taken six more. And all the A+ papers have been replaced with the report card that shows the cumulative measure of his work so far. Only keep the really precious things that will mean something in a year or ten.

When it comes to keeping your children's belongings in order, stick to limits and routines. These simple strategies will help you and your children see the value in what is kept. They will help you teach your children to be more serious about the value of what they have and how important it is. You can't keep everything, but what you do keep will be important and valuable mementos that you and they will treasure.

———

Now that the kid's rooms are clean and clutter free, how does it feel?

_____

How do your children feel about their new, cleaner and less-cluttered rooms?

_____

Along with your child make the commitment, right here and now, to keep the room looking as it does at this moment.

We will commit to taking care of this room by doing the following:

Daily: Make bed, clothes in hamper, shoes in closet, if something is taken out, it is put away.

Weekly: Empty wastebasket, dust, vacuum, wash bed linens and laundry.

Seasonally: Discard outgrown or unusable clothing and shoes.

Yearly: Stand outside the room and reassess its ideal function. Is it still achieving its ideal function? If not, what's getting in the way? Are the furniture, decoration, and playthings still age appropriate?

6

Family and Living Rooms

THERE IS NO ROOM in the house where people's ideas and visions for the space intersect as much as they do in the family room. The problem is that in being everything to everyone, this room can very easily end up with no focus at all. Instead, it becomes the center of clutter and disorganization for everyone in the family.

By talking through what family members want and expect from this space, you can give purpose to the purposeless room and in doing so redefine your family and how it uses common space. Get out your vision boards and refer back to the original questions you all answered about the functions of each of the rooms in your house. If you didn't answer those questions, now is the time to do it:

• How do we imagine using the space?

Self _____

Spouse/Partner _____

Child _____

Child _____

Child _____

• How are our visions similar? Where are they most different?

_____

_____

• How can we make it work for everyone?

_____

_____

_____

You should already have done a fast purge of this room in the house so it will be ready as you get down to the nitty-gritty.

_____

THINK IT THROUGH

Don't overload this room with too many functions. Space permitting, the room can serve a reasonable number of purposes well, but if you expect too much you run the risk of it becoming the catch-all room for the whole family—in other words, Clutter Central!

SET IT UP

Now, let's take a minute and pull together all the hard work and thought you have put into envisioning your ideal living room/family room. Write it down here as a touchstone for the work you are about to do to get this room in shape.

Goals (from page 32): _____

Ideal function (from page 46): _____

What has to go (from page 56): _____

_____

What it should contain (from page 58): _____

_____

MAKE IT HAPPEN

Everyone who uses the room should write down their responses to the following questions:

• How do I feel when I enter this room?

_____

• How do I *want* to feel when we enter this room?

_____

• What is getting in the way of the feeling I want to have?

_____

- What is this room's function for me now?

  _____

- What is the function I want it to have?

  _____

- In order to serve its function, what should the room contain in terms of furniture, contents, and open space?

  Furniture: _____

  Contents: _____

  Open space: _____

- Does each item in this room enhance and advance the vision we have for the life we want?

  _____

MAPPING THE ZONES

The greatest temptation with a family room or living room is to fill it to the brim! This is unfortunate because of all rooms in the house, this is usually the one where everyone hangs out and relaxes and the room where you need as much space as possible.

Because you will be moving things off shelves and possibly rearranging furniture to create your zones, take this opportunity to clean behind the media unit and under the couch. Get the rug, carpet, or floor cleaned. Think about repainting. A fresh coat of paint to go with the fresh start in the family room sounds like a great idea!

There's no getting around it: Watching TV or movies or playing electronic or board games is a major pastime and the family room is where this usually takes place. The whole family has a stake in this room and should have some input on how it is used. To make the room work for everyone, each family member should think about the question: *How do I want to spend my time in this room?*

Common uses for family rooms include:
- TV/video/DVD watching.
- Music.
- Electronic games.
- Board games.
- Toys.
- Crafts.
- Reading (books, magazines).
- Collectibles.
- Photos.
- _____ (Other).

Using different colored pens or pencils, each family member should put a check mark next to the activity or activities they most want to engage in while in this room. If there's a consensus (everyone marks the same thing), then that activity and corresponding furniture/equipment will become the focal point of the room. If you don't all agree, then the room will need to be portioned out differently in order to accommodate everyone's needs and interests. And make sure what people want to do in this room is appropriate for the room. Don't have weightlifting equipment in front of the TV unless you live alone.

- What is the consensus on how this space is to be used?

_____

- What is getting in the way of this space being used in the way we imagine?

_____

- What needs to be done or changed to use the space in that way?

_____

Now, look at what is already in the room and take an inventory of furniture, shelving, storage, etc. List everything here:

_____	_____
_____	_____
_____	_____
_____	_____
_____	_____

Check off the items that are compatible with how the family has decided to use the room. Are there things that do not fit the ways the family wants to use the room? Those things need to go. Toss them, sell them, or give them away. Resist the urge to "save them" for the next house or your next life. You are working this hard for *this* life, right now. Make your vision happen.

To maintain a neat and useful space it is important to keep like things together within their specific zones. All DVDs and CDs should be close to the entertainment unit. Magazines belong in a magazine rack next to your favorite chair. You should only have this month's magazines. Not six months of old magazines that you are hoping to read. Trust me, if you haven't read them by now, you won't be reading them. Electronic equipment goes in one single cabinet or shelving unit. Board games go in storage bins next to or under the coffee table where you most often play them. Or consider stashing them in an ottoman that doubles as a storage container.

The multiple remote controls can be hard to keep a handle on. Consider getting a universal remote or label all the remotes and keep them in one drawer of a side table or in a small basket under the coffee table. Teach everyone in the house where they go when viewing or playing is over for the day. Think of the time you will save no longer searching for the remote under the sofa cushions!

ENTERTAINMENT—TV, VIDEOS, DVDs, CDs, ELECTRONIC GAMES, BOOKS, AND MORE!

If you can't find the movie you want to watch or the music you want to listen to, you will find yourself becoming increasingly stressed at a time when you were ready for some relaxation and entertainment. The solution to clutter in general and decreasing stress in the family room is to ensure that all media have a clearly defined area.

DVDs

How many do you have? _____

Where do you keep them? (shelves, floor, cabinet) _____

Touch each DVD in your collection and ask, "When was the last time we watched this?" _____

Write down the number you haven't watched in the last six months _____

Take a close look at kid's tapes and DVDs—do you still have preschool shows or movies that your child or children have outgrown? Here's a hint: if you still have VHS tapes of kid's shows, your child has outgrown them.

If you have a great collection of award-winning movies, that is one thing, but if it has been more than six months since a DVD has been watched, or if it has been outgrown either by age or by interest you seriously need to consider letting it go.

Once you've gotten to the titles you really watch, here's how to keep them in order.

- Arrange them in specific categories or genres. If they came off a specific spot on the shelf, they need to go back to that specific spot.
- Clearly label the shelves or storage unit you choose so that everyone knows where the DVDs belong.
- Continue to edit what you've got. Toss, donate, sell, or give away any DVDs that you no longer want to watch.
- Once you are close to or at the limit you've set for your movie collection, if a new DVD comes in, then an old DVD needs to go out.
- Only buy what you *know* you will watch repeatedly. There is no reason to buy a DVD to watch once. In that case you can rent and return it at minimum cost and with none of the clutter guilt when you still have it on your shelf two years later.

Videos

- Have you got outdated videos taking up valuable space on your shelf?
- Are you holding onto videos when you no longer use the VHS player? Have you already got a DVD of that favorite video? Then it is time to let the video go.
- If you have home movies on video, then get the highlights transferred to DVDs so you can watch and enjoy.

Game discs and cartridges

How many game discs or cartridges do you have? _____

Where is the player/console? _____

Where are the games kept? _____

When was the last time you played each one? _____

If you've cleared the game, is there any reason to keep it any longer? _____

Again, weed out what you no longer play and enjoy. (If it hasn't been played in the last six months or the kids have outgrown it—get rid of it.)

Here's how to keep your games in order.

- Arrange by category. If you have different ages using one game player, be sure it is clear which games are for which age.
- Store them on a designated shelf or in a clearly labeled container or box.
- If you buy a new game, then an old one needs to go to make space for it.

Music

How many CDs do you have? _____

Where are they? (shelf, drawer, container, cabinet) _____

When was the last time you listened to each one? (Hint: if you can't remember, it may be time to let it go . . .) _____

Do you have any duplicates in your collection? (sorting by group/artist will reveal this to you quickly) _____

Here's how to maintain your music:

- It is usually easiest to find music on CDs if they are arranged alphabetically by group/artist. However, you might want to separate out kids' music or recorded books so they are more accessible to those who most use them.

- Weed out what you no longer listen to. Pass them on to charity, to someone who secretly dances around her home to disco in her underwear, or to a store that sells secondhand discs. Do the same for any duplicates you have in your collection.

- Go digital. Consider using software like iTunes to manage your music from your desktop or laptop. The Windows Media Center PC is also a great way to consolidate all of your music in one place. Be sure to regularly do backups of your music in the case your system crashes. Once you get a digital version, do you still need to keep the CD?

- Put your CDs in binders that will hold and protect them and their liner notes. Discard the jewel cases and see how much space you have saved.

- Once you've reached the limit of space you've assigned for your music collection, if a new CD comes in, then an old one needs to go out.

BOOKS AND MAGAZINES

Books and magazines are almost always a part of the clutter problem in homes that I see. When I encounter someone who is struggling with too many books or journals or magazines in their home or office I always ask: *What was it that you were purchasing when you bought this reading material?* This may sound like a strange question but the answer is very revealing.

Books represent different things to different people. For some they are light entertainment, for others a resource of knowledge and learning, and for others they are reminders of important moments or academic successes. However, when you buy a book you do not suddenly own the wisdom it contains—all you have bought is words on paper. It's up to you to internalize whatever enlightenment the book has to offer. Without grasping this concept it can be close to impossible to separate a person from his books.

How many books can you have?

When it comes down to it, there is only one simple rule when dealing with books. If they don't fit on your shelves, they shouldn't be in your home. Remember the Math of Stuff (page 64)?

I repeat: You should have no more than the number of books that fit comfortably *on your bookshelves*. Do not stack them on the floor or on top of the entertainment unit or in boxes in the garage. If your books don't fit on the shelving you have, you have too many. You need to either increase your shelving or cut down the number of books. It's probably no surprise that my first recommendation is not to get more shelving!

Where are your books now? _____

How many do not fit on your current shelves? _____

How many books are "waiting" to be read? _____

How many of the books are from a college course you took years ago or an interest you've long neglected or abandoned? _____

How many paperbacks? _____

How many hardcovers? _____

How many coffee table books? _____

Go to your bookshelves and do the following:

- Go through, book by book, taking each off the shelf and really looking at what you've got. (While you are at it, have a dust cloth in hand and take care of dusting the shelf at the same time.)

- Remove the books that you intended to read, but realistically won't (it's easy to have "wish" books too!).
- Remove the books that you have read, but will never read again.
- Remove the books that you read and enjoyed and can pass on to someone else.
- Keep the books you refer to again and again, or reread, or are the next books on your book club's list.
- Give the books you no longer need to a local library, shelter, school, or charity of your choice.
- When you put the books back on your shelf, you should organize them so you can find what you need. You can organize alphabetically by author or group together by genre as long as you have designated spots for each book and the system works for you.

You may find that reducing the number of books you own is easier said than done. Try to see the book purge as a way of creating a space conducive to reading and the acquisition of knowledge in a way that showcases the volumes you love and honors the collection you have.

Magazines

Can you believe there are more than 22,000 magazine titles printed in the United States? I can—having been in some homes with three years of back issues of every single one of those 22,000 magazines piled in the family room! Well, at least it seemed that way at the time.

If magazine clutter is your problem, there are some very straightforward ways of dealing with it.

Magazine management

You should have *no more than three monthly* magazine subscriptions. This may sound tough, but I have yet to meet the person who can deal with the amount of reading material in three magazine subscriptions on

WHAT TO DO WITH BOOKS, DVDs, VIDEOS, VIDEO GAMES, AND CDs

- Used books, DVDs, and CDs can all be donated to a library, school, or charity.
- Sell them at a tag sale. Sell them to a used book store. Sell them online.
- Join a site like Swap Tree (*SwapTree.com*) for free exchange/trade of books, DVDs, videos, and CDs.

top of busy work schedules, a family, the daily newspaper, competing media, and just plain living!

Keep those magazines *not* coming!

- Avoid committing to an automatic renewal of your subscriptions—it's so easy to do. You will probably have had the subscription at least six months before the renewal notices start to come so you will know whether you actually are reading and enjoying the magazine. If you are, check your mailing label to find out when your subscription actually runs out, that date is when you should resubscribe. If you have not read last month's magazine and chose instead to recycle it, let the subscription lapse.
- Don't fall for the renew now mailings and flyers that offer super discounts or your subscription will outlast you! Be honest, if the magazines are piling up, no matter how cheap the renewal is, you are not saving anything.

You can save a tree (or three) by stopping the flow of magazines into your home. It's time to take a hard look at one of the biggest sources of clutter in the family room and around the house.

Do you know how many magazine subscriptions you receive? To really

Magazine	How many issues do you have right now?	When was the last time you read a full issue?	Could you recycle it right now without losing sleep?
Newsweek	_____	_____	_____
Vogue	_____	_____	_____
People	_____	_____	_____
_____	_____	_____	_____
_____	_____	_____	_____
_____	_____	_____	_____

get a sense of what magazines are coming into your house make a list here. Don't forget all family members' subscriptions—including the kids. Now that you have a list of the magazines that are coming into your home on a regular basis, are there any that provide duplicate information? Do you need two newsweeklies? How much celebrity/fashion/style can you read about? Do you get magazines about hobbies or activities that you no longer engage in? Consider if you can get the information easily online and either subscribe or bookmark the appropriate sites on your computer.

Getting a handle on the magazines coming in doesn't stop there. Once you've determined the magazines that you do want to spend your time with you need to come up with a system for preventing them taking over every available surface in your home and building up into one big pile of guilt.

Magazine rules

1. Have a designated spot for magazines. This could be a magazine rack, a basket, or bin. You can only hold onto the magazines that fit in this container.

2. Never keep more than two past issues of any one magazine

around—particularly weeklies. When the third comes in, the first issue goes out. (If the third issue comes and you haven't read the earlier issues this may be a subscription you need to cancel or let lapse.)

3. If you are keeping an entire issue for one article, cut or tear it out and put it in a folder or your pocket or your bag so you can read it on the go.
4. If you are keeping an entire issue for a recipe, cut or tear it out and collect it in a folder or binder and create a cookbook of your very own.
5. Once you have read—recycle!

Cutting off the catalogs

Catalogs are another source of clutter in family rooms. They can be fun to page through but if they are allowed to overstay their welcome they can contribute an enormous amount of clutter. Here is how to get a handle on catalogs:

1. Get a cardboard box. Every time a catalog comes in the mail toss it in the box.
2. After three weeks you will be amazed at how many catalogs have accumulated.
3. Take a look at what is coming into your home. Are there catalogs from a company you ordered from once, but won't again? Are you getting catalogs for infant developmental toys when the kids are already in college?
4. Sort the catalogs into two piles. Will Order From and Won't Order From.
5. Take the Won't Order From pile, call the 800 numbers, and ask to be taken off the catalog list. It may take a couple of issues to stop but it will.
6. Take a close look at the Will Order From pile. How often do you really order? If it is pretty consistent, OK, let the catalogs continue.

If not, get back on the phone and get yourself off of that list as well. All major retailers now have websites, and it's easier to visit the site when you need something than have to recycle the catalog every month when you don't.

7. See page 159, Strategies for Minimizing Junk Mail.
8. Always recycle magazines and catalogs.

COLLECTIBLE OR CLUTTER?

Collectibles are so not because of what they're worth or who owns them but because of the pleasure and joy and value they bring to you. There is a thin line between collectibles and clutter though, and it is very easy for both to take over your home: In your mind you may be a collector, but in reality you may be a hoarder.

People seem to collect everything from Pez dispensers to fine china. While I'll concede that "collectability" is often in the eye of the beholder, in actual fact the line between collectible and clutter is razor thin. In-

REALITY CHECK—COLLECTIONS

It's a collection if:

- it's displayed in a way that makes you proud and shows that you value and honor it.
- looking at it brings you pleasure.
- you enjoy showing it to others.
- it is not an obsession that is damaging your relationships.
- it is not buried under other clutter.
- it doesn't get in the way of living the life you wish you had.

creasingly, people use the word "collectible" like a "get out of jail free" card—it's become an excuse to hold onto whatever they want. My position is simple—calling a group of like things "a collection" does not automatically give them value or provide a reason for holding onto them.

There are four questions that need to be asked to solve the clutter versus collectible conundrum:

1. Do these items reinforce the vision I have for myself, my home, and my family?
2. Do these items deserve the value I am placing on them by having them front and center in my home?
3. If I say I value them, am I showing that value by how I use or display the items?
4. Is my collection coming between myself and my family?

If you answered "No" to any of the first three questions or yes to question four, why are you still holding on to those items? They are baggage and they are getting in the way of your happiness. Get rid of them now.

It's all about looking at your things with fresh eyes and determining if you are filling your home with things you value or simply filling your home.

Heirlooms

Sometimes we hold onto things we have or things we have been given (heirlooms) in the hope that they will be valuable some day. What you have may be worth something. Or not. But you'll never know unless you take some action. Don't let china or other items take up valuable space in your home "in case" it is worth something. Find out! It may take a little legwork or a few Internet searches, but you can get an idea of the value of silver, china, art, decorative items, clothes, electronics, jewelry, or other items with a little time spent online. With china and silver it is helpful to know the manufacturer as well as the pattern name of the piece in order to assess value. Believe me, for almost every collectible there is a website or book dedicated to identifying and pricing it.

Several resources are available to help you determine a ballpark value:

- eBay—one of the biggest marketplaces in the world. You can discover here what your possessions are worth on the open market. If that "valuable" figurine you inherited from your grandmother is selling for $9.99 on eBay, then it is time to wake up and smell the coffee and lose the figurine.
- Web search—can give information about objects and help to identify them and get a sense of their worth.
- Library and/or bookstore—has reference materials that can give information about objects and help to identify them, which can lead to determining worth.

Armed with the manufacturer's name and the pattern name or number you can find out much about the relative value of your pieces. Remember, however, that especially with objects like china or silver the age and condition will be a factor in determining price. Some auction houses will help you to identify an object if you send a photo but usually an item must be seen in person to give a true appraisal of its worth.

If you are keeping something because you think it might be worth something—find out and either put it in place of pride or sell it and get some money for it. Only don't use that money as an excuse to go out get more questionable collectibles! If you love it, display it or use it in a way that clearly demonstrates that you value it.

Emotional value versus real worth

Another key evaluation when it comes to collectibles and decorative items is their emotional value versus their real worth. Does knowing the real value influence how you feel about an item? If your home was threatened by fire and your family and pets were all OK and you had time to take ten items out of the family room, what would they be?

What ten items would you take?

_____   _____

_____   _____

_____   _____

_____   _____

Are these ten items used or displayed or stored in a way that shows the value you place on them? _____

_____

Why not? _____

What do you need to do or change to display or store them appropriately?

_____

Be honest, what ten items could you leave behind without a second thought?

_____   _____

_____   _____

_____   _____

_____   _____

Why are they still in your home?

_____

What are you going to do with them now?

_____

How does it feel to get rid of them?

_____

BOARD GAMES, TOYS, CRAFTS

In order for the family to enjoy the space you have set aside for family activities, they need to have the elbow room to do so. Designate spots for game playing or crafting or playing with toys. Again, it is a matter of keeping the supplies nearest to where you will use them—and returning them to their proper spot after play or use.

Just as with other rooms in the house, you need to assess what you have, how often you use it, and how it fits your vision of your life in your home.

Board games

List the games you have here:

_____

_____

Who plays them? _____

How often? _____

If a game hasn't been touched in the last six months, ask yourself if it's time for it to go. Use this as an opportunity to discard any games that are broken, missing pieces, or are otherwise unplayable. Also, see what the kids have outgrown, either by age or interest, and pass those games (in good condition) on to someone who will enjoy them.

Toys

If toys share the space in the living/family room they must be brought under the same scrutiny as all else in the house. Look back at the section on cleaning kids' rooms for advice on how to clear out and store toys.

Crafts, hobbies, scrapbooking

These items should be in your family room only if this room is the only place in the house they can be stored. And *only* if they do not interfere with how everyone is using this room.

I have seen rooms overrun with the tools and materials needed for crafting, hobbies, and scrapbooking. In many cases, there is good intention behind embarking on an activity (*I can do a scrapbook of baby's first year!*) but those intentions often vanish in the face of daily life and its demands. Ultimately hobbies can become more wishful thinking than enjoyable activity. If you are serious about your hobbies and they bring you joy, *and* you have some place to exhibit the finished project, then make sure that the materials do not overwhelm the room or overwhelm you so you don't know where to start or where you left off. Another thing you can do is pick one project. Put everything not associated with that project away and work on that one item until you are finished. Don't hop from project to project. You will never finish anything, your materials will be scattered and easily lost, and you will get frustrated and abandon something that made you happy.

SENTIMENTAL ITEMS

Do you have trouble letting go of items to which you have given sentimental value? Your grandmother's mildewed wedding dress? Your father's dress blues? Your babies' first blankets? One idea to save the memory but not the clutter is to cut out a piece of the fabric and frame it in a shadowbox next to a photo of the person wearing or using the article. Write out your memory of that person or that moment and hang the box on the wall in a place where everyone can see and enjoy it.

Another thing to do with fabric items—but *only* if you will use the final product and if saving the items will not lead to clutter—is to cut up whatever items matter to you: old clothes, yours, your children's, or family hand-me-downs, to make a memory quilt. It will last a long time and bring back those memories—without clogging your drawers and closets with items you can no longer wear or use.

FAMILY PHOTOS

We all take photos but few of us are photographers. You're lucky if a tenth of the photos you take are quality photos. Here's what you do.

1. Get a nice photo album.
2. For every event you go to—wedding, family outing, weekend getaway—pick the best photo of the lot and put it in the album.
3. Next to it, on a piece of paper, write a paragraph about the event.
4. Put the album in a public, prominent place, like the coffee table in your family room.

5. That album becomes a greatest hits collection of important events. An album like this is a pleasure to look through, for you and for your visitors.

Of course, if you can go digital, by all means do so. You'll quickly see how infrequently you actually bother to look at your photos, even when they're right there on your computer taking up no physical space in your home whatsoever. (Remember to back up your computer so the photos do not get lost.) There are also various web-based companies (Shutterfly, Snapfish) that enable you to upload your digital photos and have them made into beautiful bound albums.

Photos of children and children's artwork

Kids grow quickly and you want to record every minute of their growing up that you can. This leads to a lot of video and photos that you can't display and are hard to store. Try the photo album idea above for most of the photos. There will be some photos you want to display, and below are some ideas on how to do that without being overrun by every picture you take of Johnnie, Susie, and Joanie.

1. Choose a few easy-to-use frames.
2. Hang them in a prominent spot in your home.
3. Fill them with your current favorite snapshot or piece of art.
4. Every few months, swap in a new photo or painting.
5. Move the retired favorite to an album.
6. You can do the same thing by slipping photos under Plexiglas on your desk.
7. Use a photo as the desktop on your computer or create a slideshow of photos as your screensaver.
8. Get a digital frame that cycles your photos for you. When you take new pictures, just upload the new photos to replace the old ones.

You should store videos of family events with your entertainment items near the TV. Label them clearly, categorize them so they are easy to find. Since you may not watch these videos frequently but will still want to watch them years from now, you'll need to store them safely so they won't get damaged.

Congratulations, you have reclaimed yet another room in your home from the clutches of clutter. It's hard work to make a multipurpose room serve the family and their ideal for that room, but you have done it!

SPACE BENEFITS

The less clutter you have in your home, the more you can reap the benefits of free space. Now your family can sit down at the dining room table and enjoy a meal together. Now your family room is a comfortable place to relax. Now you can have friends over or host a spontaneous party. Gone is the shame and embarrassment of having a home that bears no resemblance to the one you want to present to the world. Revel in your space. Host parties. Show off! You've earned it.

Now that the family room/living room is clean and clutter free, how does it feel? Get everyone to weigh in here because everyone is benefiting from the new room and will need to commit to keeping it clear and clean.

Make the commitment, right here and now to keep it looking as it does at this moment.

I will commit to taking care of this room by doing the following:

Daily: If something is taken out, it is put away, Five-Minute Purge.

Weekly: Empty waste paper basket, dust, vacuum, be sure that all media is back where it belongs.

Monthly: Assess what games, toys, DVDs, and/or CDs haven't been used, watched, or listened to. Assess if the clutter is still out of the room.

Seasonal: Move furniture away from the walls and really clean; take the opportunity to fix or replace broken or damaged furniture; possibly switch curtains or slipcovers for the new season.

Yearly: Stand outside the room and reassess its ideal function and if it is still achieving that ideal function. What's getting in the way?

7

Home Office

THE HOME OFFICE has become a standard area in many homes. Many people use this space to work from home, to handle the day-to-day business of running a household, to answer mail and pay bills, and as a place for their computers. While we'd all like the home office to be a model of efficiency, for many it seems to be a special kind of magnet that attracts every piece of paper that comes into the home: books, magazines, bills, receipts, tax necessities, product warranties, letters, files, and reams of personal "must-keep" data that has no clear home other than on a desk, chair, or the floor in the corner of the room.

THINK IT THROUGH

Office clutter is almost always a paper problem. What's amazing is that if you think about the paper that fills your office—the books, magazines, files, and mail—you'll realize that you'll never use or need most of it again. As we work on the paper problem areas, you'll learn to assess how much of that paper to keep and how it is best kept. Go back to your vision board and the first round of questions before you start on this room. Include everyone who uses this room on a regular basis in the cleanup. Write down your responses to the following questions:

- How do I feel when I enter my home office?

  _____

- How do I *want* to feel when I enter this room?

  _____

- What is this room's function now?

  _____

- What is the function I want it to have?

  _____

- In order to serve its function, what should the room contain in terms of furniture, contents, and open space?

Furniture: _____

Contents: _____

Open space: _____

- Does each item in this room enhance and advance the vision I have for the life I want?

_____

_____

SET IT UP

Now, let's take a minute and pull together all the hard work and thought you have put into envisioning your ideal home office. Write it down here as a touchstone for the work you are about to do to get this room in shape.

Goals (from page 32): _____

Ideal function (from page 46): _____

What has to go (from page 56): _____

_____

What it should contain (from page 58)

_____

_____

MAKE IT HAPPEN

As you are moving items from your desk and out of drawers, take the opportunity to clean all surfaces and clean out the drawers. An office makeover may require a coat of paint or a deep clean of the carpet or rug.

Also, you want to be sure you have storage on the desk for those items that you need immediate access to. Be sure you have a pen and

FINANCIAL BENEFITS OF A CLUTTER-FREE LIFE

When you organize your papers, your financial life improves. Bills are paid on time. You can work toward paying off debt. Not only that, when you start looking at all the stuff you own but don't use or appreciate, it should help you buy fewer items and spend less money. When you spend less time shopping, you spend more time finding new interests, being active in the outdoors, being with your family and friends.

pencil holder which next to the message pad which is close to the phone. If this is used as a real office on a daily basis you should think about what supplies you need on top of the desk. Magnetic dispensers/holders for paperclips, small dispensers for sticky notes, and an inbox/to-do box, tape, scissors, stapler are all items that can make your desk function better. They can also lead to clutter if you are not using them so be clear about how you use this room and your desk while you are clearing your desk out.

Be sure your computer monitor and hard drive are on a stable surface and you use a surge protector to plug them in. Standing file organizers or stackable paper trays can keep paper and other items controlled. Cord-snakes or cord guards can bundle cords from multiple electronics together and make them less unsightly as well as reduce the tripping hazard.

MAPPING THE ZONES

A home office can serve a number of functions and should have designated places to fulfill those functions. The typical home office serves as a place for:

- Mail.
- Bill paying.
- Files.
- Reading.
- Studying.
- Computer work.

Central to a home office will be a desk. The type of desk you choose isn't as important as the fact that it will accommodate the uses you intend for it. Is there ample space for your computer, phone, pens, pencils, light, calendar, paper, and other items? If more than one person is using the desk is there adequate space for each person to do what they need to do?

The desk

List the uses you envision for your desk: _____

_____

_____

List items you need to fulfill the ideal function of the desk: _____

_____

_____

List what is presently on your desk: _____

_____

_____

List what is in your desk (drawer by drawer): _____

_____

_____

Are the things both on and in your desk essential to how you want and need to use your desk? _____

_____

Take away the things that do not belong (anything that isn't essential to the ideal function of the desk). Get rid of duplicate items, such as two rulers. Make sure that all pens actually work—toss those that are out of ink. Get rid of pencils stubs, the calendar from five years ago, the broken stapler, sticky notes that have lost their stick. Collect paperclips and store them together; collect rubber bands and store them together. Reclaim the space for what it is meant for.

From now on, keep all horizontal spaces clear. If you don't start piles, they can't grow.

Home offices are usually paper central and paper can lead to lots of clutter if not handled efficiently and effectively. Make sure that you have designated places (file folders and files, bins or baskets, hanging files) for the main types of paper that lives in this space:

- Mail.
- Bills and receipts.
- Important personal information and files.
- Magazines.

Mail

We all receive important information through the mail, and much of it requires some kind of response to ensure the smooth running of our homes and our lives. Bills need to be paid, invitations require a response, and inquiries from the bank or a government office need replies.

As soon as the mail comes into the house sort it as close to a recycling bin as possible. Immediately toss junk mail, unwanted catalogs, flyers, promotional mailings—anything you do not need or want. Doing this is like a Five-Minute Purge of your mail.

Another strategy is to stop the junk mail from ever reaching your home. This is a little more time consuming but well worth the effort.

Once you've got your mail down to the bare essentials, you can sort it for each family member. (A mail sorter with slots for each person in your

STRATEGIES FOR MINIMIZING JUNK MAIL

✓ Contact the Direct Marketing Association by email or regular mail. Visit their website DMAchoice.org. For the purposes of their site, direct mail is divided into four categories, Credit Offers, Catalogs, Magazine Offers, and Other Mail Offers. You can request to start or stop receiving mail from individual companies within each category—or from an entire category at once. Or send a postcard to *DMAChoice, Direct Marketing Association, P.O. Box 643, Carmel, New York, 10512.* Ask them to "*activate the mail preference service.*" You need to list your complete name, address, and zip code. Listing with the mail preference service will stop 75 percent of all national mailings. It may take a couple of months before you notice a difference in the volume of junk mail, but it is well worth doing it now.

✓ Avoid receiving all of those annoying credit card offers that swamp all of us. Call toll-free, 24 hours a day: 888.567.8688 (888.5OPT.OUT) to have your name removed from the list of the major credit organizations. Follow the computer prompts and choose to have your name removed for two years or forever. You can also opt out online by going to OptOutPrescreen.com.

✓ Insist that your name and address not be sold when you sign up for a new catalog, buy a new product, or any time you provide your personal details as part of a business transaction. Save a tree, control the clutter, and save a little sanity. Every little bit helps!

✓ There are also paid mailer removal services:

41pounds.org (named after the weight of junk mail the average adult receives annually). The service costs $41.00 for five years.

home is a handy way to do this. This sorter can also be used for any phone messages or notes family members need to give to each other.

Bills

Bills are the most important mail we receive. If bills are not paid on time credit card companies have no hesitation in slapping you with late fees or higher interest rates. If utility bills are left unpaid you can find yourself without a phone or other basic services. If school bills are not paid, your kids could be asked to leave school. If your mortgage and taxes aren't paid, you risk losing your home.

Not being on top of your bills costs in ways beyond the financial. It causes stress and tension, both for you and others in your household. It can seriously impact your reputation and your credit rating. In the long run, it can jeopardize your ability in the future to take major loans for a home or a car.

If you pay your bills in your office, keep your checkbook, stamps, a pen, envelopes, and a calculator in one location on your desk in a basket, tray, or bin. When bills come in, place them in that container. Set aside a time to pay the bills and make it the same day and time each week. You will have all you need at hand to pay your bills on time and effectively.

My bill paying day and time will be _____

Alternatively, to save paper and time, many bills can be paid electronically. Once you've set up your account to be paid electronically, you can

CREDIT CARD DEBT

It may not seem obvious, but there is a connection between debt and clutter. I'm not talking about home, school, or car loans. Those loans tend to have reasonable interest rates, but credit card debt is a real devil, and it is always the result of inappropriate acquisition of goods. You see a beautiful cashmere sweater on sale and you have to have it, now! It doesn't matter that you can't afford it or that you have nowhere to wear it, or that you already have three beautiful cashmere sweaters. In your eyes, that sweater will change your life. But then when you get your credit card bill, if you can't pay it in full, that bargain starts to cost more and more each month with the fees you are paying. Once you've got a little debt, it's a hard habit to break. The average American family owes $9,200 in credit card debt and that number will continue to grow.

When it comes to managing your credit cards, you need to establish routines and set limits. Sound familiar? It's the same thing I told you to teach your children. Limited space equals limited toys. Limited funds equals limited spending. Trust me, no matter how much you want that stereo or that appliance upgrade, excess spending will bring you more grief than that immediate gratification is worth.

pay bills in minutes, save paper, and save a stamp! Consider software like Quicken to track all bills, assist in online payments, and help in the yearly preparation of your taxes. Most companies will accept an automatic bill paying schedule, or you can simply set up your online account and then check the bills to ensure their accuracy each month before approving the money transfer.

Filing

The key to keeping on top of filing is to have a designated space for files and a system so you can easily find what you are looking for.

Be aware that file cabinets can be sneaky. They masquerade as organization solutions, but while they're better than random stacks of disorderly papers they don't automatically solve the problem. Why? Because part of the problem, strangely, is that a file cabinet can hold so much paper that the temptation is to fill it, or to file everything. This is a mistake! Remember that 80 percent of what goes into a filing cabinet never sees the light of day again. Be judicious about what you file and schedule a time each year (tax time is a good one) to go through your files and get rid of those things that are outdated or no longer needed.

Go through your file cabinet drawer by drawer and then file by file. Have a large trash bag handy and clear a place on your desktop for personal items you will want to rip up or shred.

Start with A and pull out everything in that file. Ask yourself "Why am I holding onto this information?" Immediately toss anything that is outdated or does not contain personal information. You can toss out ancient receipts, warranties or instruction booklets for items you no longer have, birthday or holiday cards, and so on. On the desktop put anything that needs to be shredded. (See below for guidelines on keeping certain financial and tax documents.)

The things you will be returning to your newly cleaned out file cabinet will have importance to your life and serve as a record of useful information.

Invest in a good filing system

Use a stable, well-made filing cabinet and consider one of the commercially available systems like File Solutions or Freedom Filer (see Resources section for information) that help to keep paperwork in order by providing pre-labeled files that cover every conceivable aspect of home operation. These systems organize and manage your personal and family papers and take any guesswork out of setting up an easy-to-use and complete system.

Clearly label your files (a label maker is a great tool for this purpose) in a logical way that enables you to quickly and efficiently retrieve any information you need. If you're ambitious, color-code them like the professionals do—whatever you do, choose a system that will work for your particular situation. Once you file something it can be very easy to forget where it is, or even that it exists. A good filing system ensures that you can quickly and confidently lay your hands on any important paperwork without raising a sweat.

Suggested filing categories

Automotive—maintenance and repair details, warranties, purchase details.

Education—copies of transcripts or degrees. Report cards, school details. (Consider making subfolders for each family member.)

Financial—credit cards, bank statements, investments, retirement funds. (Create subfolders for the various companies and institutions.)

Health and medical—details of coverage, medical practitioner contact information, any special medical or dental records.

Home real estate—house purchase details, tax records, copies of receipts for work done on property, investment property details.

Household products—receipts, instruction manuals, and warranties for large household items.

Insurance—house and contents policies, car insurance, life insurance, disability insurance, or any other policies you may have. Paperwork related to any claims you have filed.

Legal—important documents such as passports, birth and marriage certificates, copies of wills and trusts. These items might be better placed in a fireproof box or cabinet.

Work—employment contracts, resumes, work benefit program details.

Taxes—one file for each year's return and supporting paperwork.

Just because you have a great system it doesn't mean you have to file every piece of paper that comes your way. When a bank statement comes, clear out the ATM receipts from your wallet or purse, match them to the statement, and then discard (or shred) them. When your credit card bill comes, match the receipts to the bill and discard (or shred) the receipts. Only keep credit card receipts for tax, warranty, or insurance purposes.

Be efficient
- The top drawer of your filing cabinet should contain the files you need the most, including receipts, bank statements, and other paperwork you'll want for this year's tax return.
- Store old tax files in a less accessible place. You'll only need them again if you're audited.
- Consider assigning a drawer to each family member and maintaining one drawer for common paperwork.
- Make labels for the outside of each drawer of your filing cabinet so you can see at a glance what that drawer contains.

Alternatives to the file cabinet

Sometimes a file cabinet may not be the best solution to all your filing needs. There is a simple, low-tech solution I use and recommend for the paperwork that is left on your desk after you pay your bills each month. Try investing in a twelve-month expanding file, which is divided into twelve sections by month. Then, when you pay your bills each month, keep the stubs in this expanding file. Placing paid bills into their corresponding month is a simple and effective way to keep a record of what's been paid. When you come around to that month in a year's time, if you haven't needed to refer to those paid bills—which is highly likely—then shred or discard them. This can also be a great solution for monthly receipts or other pesky paperwork that you're unsure whether or not you'll need to refer to in the immediate future.

The tax man

The concern that Uncle Sam may come knocking to conduct a tax audit strikes fear into our hearts. Keeping your financial records in order and knowing that the supporting documents are easily accessible should allay that fear enormously. The government provides clear guidelines for what records we need to keep—it's our job to make sure we're organized enough to meet those standards and it's really not that difficult to do.

Here are some broad and fairly conservative guidelines for managing your bills and financial records for tax season and audits. My official disclaimer is that you shouldn't take my word for it and should check with

IRS SPECIFICATIONS

You can download a publication of the IRS about what paperwork to keep. Go to irs.gov and search for Publication No. 552.

your own accountant or financial advisor in your state to verify that this information is up-to-date and accurate for your state and situation.

TAX TRASH CALENDAR

EVERY MONTH:

- Toss out ATM and bank deposit slips and credit card receipts after you have checked them against your bank or credit card statements.
- Toss out receipts for minor purchases—unless there is a warranty or refund involved.

EVERY YEAR:

- Toss out your monthly bank and credit card statements (unless you require proof of deductions for taxation purposes)—most credit card companies provide a year-end summary that you can retain.
- Toss out monthly mortgage statements, provided you receive a year-end summary of your account.
- Toss out pay stubs after they are checked against your W-2 or 1099.
- Toss out your W-2 and 1099 forms from seven years ago and earlier.
- Toss out cancelled checks and receipts or annual statements for:

  mortgage interest from seven years ago and earlier

  property taxes from seven years ago and earlier

  deductible business expenses or other tax-deductible expenses from seven years ago and earlier

KEEP INDEFINITELY:

- Annual tax returns.
- Year-end summary statements from financial institutions.
- Receipts for the purchase of any investments you own.
- Receipts for home-improvement costs or major purchases that may be needed for insurance claims or similar.

Reading, studying, and computer work

If the home office is to be used by multiple family members, some of the usages will be reading, studying, and computer work. While your kids may have a desk in their own rooms, they may need to use the home office computer for a school project or for other research or work. Make sure that any house rules about the kids' use of the computer are followed to the letter. Back up and protect files so Junior doesn't accidentally delete important information and to ensure you have copies of files in the event of a system crash.

Digital declutter

If you are like many people you have a number of electronic devices that clamor for you attention, hold valuable information, and streamline your life, but can also be a source of digital clutter. If you have a computer, an electronic reader, a smart phone, or a cell phone, you know that electronic clutter can make information less easy to access and turn your time-saving device into one that makes your life more difficult rather than less. It pays to do a weekly Five-Minute Purge of your most used devices to rid them of what you no longer are using or need and free up space for the materials and information you do need and use.

Computers

Organize your files clearly, delete old computer files regularly, back up your important files and, wherever possible, use the Internet to conduct business, pay bills, and so on.

- When it comes to email, the fewer items in your in-box, the better. Some people think of the in-box as a to-do list—it should have only essential items that need your immediate attention.
- Be sure to have a good spam filter on your e-mail. Some services have them (check with your provider) but you can also download spam-filtering programs like Mailwasher (mailwasher.net) and SpamAssassin (spamassassin.apache.org).
- Create subfolders to group related emails.
- Archive old emails to keep those folders from becoming over-stuffed.
- Don't forget to sort through and delete emails in your in-box, deleted folder, and sent folder.

Periodically sort through your electronic devices to delete outdated messages, pictures you no longer want to hold onto, or games you no longer play. Having multiple gigabytes doesn't give you license to not monitor and pay attention to what you are carrying around with you electronically.

CORPORATE OFFICE

Your home office is often a shared space for you, your partner, and the kids. But the corporate office is yours and yours alone. It is *the* place where you conduct business and should be putting your best foot forward.

Whether you are in a cubicle or a corner office, the tools and ideas that you use in revamping your home office can work very well in the corporate environment.

Stand outside your office door and look in. Imagine that you are a client or co-worker seeing this office for the first time.

What do you see? _____

_____

_____

What image does it project?

_____

Is this the image you want to project to clients and colleagues?

_____

What image do you want to have?

_____

What is your vision for the ideal function of your office?

_____

Does this office look like a place where good, clear decisions get made?

_____

Is this office helping you achieve your vision of your ideal career?

_____

If not, what is getting in the way? Are there papers everywhere? Do piles of reports, documents, and other information threaten to topple over any minute? Can you find your in-box?

_____

Can you do the work you need to do—efficiently, effectively?

_____

What needs to change?

_____

Here, as at home, you need to develop a system for handling the paper that goes in and out of the office, take action on the items that need your attention, and file away the information as needed.

- Create a space for incoming mail (including interoffice).
- Create a space for outgoing mail (including interoffice).
- Keep a calendar (paper or electronic) to track deadlines and appointments.
- Set up files for projects or clients and maintain them (file daily or weekly; annually purge unneeded papers).
- Have a place for paper, pens, stapler, tape, etc.
- Because your computer is likely the tool you use most for conducting business, take a few minutes each day—a Five-Minute Purge—and sort, delete, and archive emails.
- Talk to you company's IT department about spam filters and how best to use them.
- Clean up your computer desktop and reduce the number of folders or documents you have there.

Just as at home, having clear spaces for relevant activities is the key to keeping your office efficient and you working at your best.

Now that the home office is clean and clutter free, how does it feel?

_____

Make the commitment, right here and now, to keep it looking as it does at this moment.

I will commit to taking care of this room by doing the following:

Daily: Sort the mail, recycle the junk. If something is taken out, put it away. Do a Five-Minute Purge.

Weekly: File, empty wastebasket, dust, vacuum, clear out email.

Monthly: Pay bills. Assess if the clutter is still out of the room.

Yearly: Purge (shred if necessary) files of outdated or unneeded papers/paperwork. Stand outside the room and reassess its ideal function. If it is not achieving its ideal function, what's getting in the way?

8

Kitchen

AFTER THE MASTER BEDROOM the kitchen is the most important room in the home. The kitchen is the heart of the home and is often where the most family action takes place—chatting, cooking, eating, maybe doing homework or even paying the bills. The kitchen counters and table can also be where everyone drops their things. Books and book bags, bills, homework, clothing, mail, and more often find their way to the table and counter. When you add all that stuff to what's already on the counter that is needed for preparing, serving, and eating meals, the kitchen can be a tough place to keep organized and clean.

If you haven't done so already, take five minutes now and do a quick surface clean so you can more easily get down to the nitty-gritty as you work over this room and return it to the ideal function of storing, serving, and eating food. And in this room the quick surface clean includes identifying the useless appliances and "display" items that are cluttering up your space and crowding your vision. They need to go.

THINK IT THROUGH

The kitchen is all about form and function. No matter how large or small, your kitchen can be highly functional. Don't let a small kitchen be your excuse for clutter. You know which pots and which pans, dishes, and implements that you use all the time. Keep what you use everyday close at hand. You need clear counter space more than you need that fondue pot you got last year. Get out your vision board and refer back to the questions you answered during the first walk-through of the house.

SET IT UP

Really doing the work on your kitchen will take two to four hours, so make sure you have that time to commit before you start. Now, let's take a minute and pull together all the hard work and thought you have put into envisioning your ideal kitchen. Write it down here as a touchstone for the work you are about to do to get this room in shape.

Goals (from page 33): _____

Ideal function (from page 46): _____

What has to go (from page 56): _____

_____

What it should contain (from page 58) _____

MAKE IT HAPPEN

Write down your responses to the following questions. Ultimately, there is always one person in the family who "owns" the kitchen, but everyone uses this room so get everyone's input too. You might be surprised.

- How do I feel when I enter the kitchen?

_____

- How do I *want* to feel when I enter this room?

_____

- What is this room's function now?

_____

- What is the function I want it to have?

_____

- In order to serve its function, what furniture, contents, and open space should the room contain?

Furniture: _____

Cabinet and drawer contents (this includes all the nonfood items, like appliances, utensils, dishes, mixing bowls, glasses—really think this one all the way down to the last wooden spoon, you'll thank me): _____

_____

_____

_____

- Does each item in this room enhance and advance the vision I have for the life I want?

_____

MAPPING YOUR ZONES

Take a good honest look at your kitchen. The kitchen is where you prepare meals for yourself and your family, where you physically nurture your partner and children. Is your kitchen someplace where you can easily prepare and enjoy healthy meals? If a neighbor popped in unexpectedly, would you be able to sit down for a cup of coffee without moving a mound of stuff? If your kids bring friends home are there healthy snacks and drinks in easy reach for them to serve themselves? If you needed to make a quick meal for your family without going to the store do you have the supplies to do that? Do you have things (appliances, food, decoration) in your kitchen that you hold onto because you hope to be the kind of person who uses them someday? Do you know where everything is in your kitchen? Your kitchen is as much a representation of you as the master bedroom and, just like that room, if the kitchen is out of order it tends to throw off the balance of every other room in the house.

See your kitchen through fresh eyes and reclaim it as the place where you feed and nurture your family. The typical kitchen zones are:

- Preparation.
- Cooking.
- Eating.
- Storage.
- Cleanup.

Preparation

The preparation area should be near the sink for quick cleanup and it should have plenty of free counter space with easy access to knives and cutting boards.

- What is currently on your counters? How much of what is there actually belongs there? And when was the last time you used what is on your counter?

_____

- Is what is on the counters getting in the way of the ideal function of this part of the kitchen? Where should those items be stored if not on the counter? Is there room to put them away or is their rightful place already stuffed with other stuff you never use?

_____

- What needs to be on your counters to serve the ideal function of your kitchen?

_____

- What is in, near, and under your sink? How long has what's under your sink been there? Honestly, how long?

_____

Sink area

You need ample room in and around your sink to prepare foods and to wash and dry any dishes or pans that don't go in the dishwasher. You should have a way to dry these items as soon as they are washed. Why keep a rack on your counter taking up space if you only use it once a day? Dry the items and put them away. Then you'll have clean dishes and a clear counter.

First of all, if you have young children at home put a childproof lock on the door under the sink to keep chemicals out of reach.

Next, get under the sink and clear it out. I know it's scary, but pull everything out. What is going on under your sink is a good indication of what is going on the rest of your kitchen. Toss out any crumbly, musty sponges, leaky rubber gloves, and empty dish soap containers. How many bottles of cleaner do you have? When was the last time you wiped the whole thing clean? Think about it if where you store your cleaning supplies is disgusting and cluttered, how clean can the rest of your kitchen really be?

Cooking

The cooking center is near the stove and needs to have easy access to pots, pans, cooking utensils, and spices. The only things that should be on your stove when it's not in use are a tea kettle and a spoon rest if you use one. The only thing that should be stored in your oven is space. As tempting as all that "unused" space in the oven can be, it is not a place to keep pots or pans. If you are storing pots and pans in your oven we have to figure out why you don't have room for them in your cabinets. Do you have too many different pots and pans? Are you storing other things in your cabinets that you don't use or need? We are going to empty your cabinets in a minute. But take a moment now to start thinking about what you are going to get rid of to make room again for your pots and pans. If your oven and stove top aren't clean and free of clutter, how will you make appetizing meals for your family and friends? Take the time now to give a good scouring to your stovetop and oven. While you are at it, clean out the toaster and/or toaster oven of all the breadcrumbs that have accumulated there. (By the way, do you really need a toaster *and* a toaster oven?) Give your microwave a good clean too. We'll get to the pots, pans, and cooking utensils in a minute. If counter space is at a premium you should consider combining appliances—a convection toaster oven cooks, toasts, and broils in the space of a toaster oven and lets you get rid of the toaster and the toaster oven. If you use a food processor once a year for pesto, a blender should probably cover all your needs. Give that big counter-hogging processor to someone who will use it.

Eating

If your eating area is in the kitchen, whether it's a table or a counter, it needs clear space and easy access to eating utensils, napkins, salt and pepper and other condiments.

- Take a look at your kitchen table. What is on it? Is what is on the table essential to eating?

_____

_____

- If not, why is it there?

_____

Remove anything from the table that is not essential to its ideal function—school books, mail, magazines, and articles of clothing. Get family members involved so they can reclaim their items and return them to their rightful place. The dining area in your kitchen should be clear of everything unless you are eating. Salt and pepper, napkins, butter, should all go back where they belong after each meal.

Storage

Both perishable and nonperishable items should be stored in such a way that you have access to them when you need them and so you can be aware of expiration dates. That way you won't waste money or run out of essential foods.

When was the last time you cleaned out your pantry or food cupboards? Not just the front row but all the way back? Well, we are going to do it today, so get ready.

• Do you find yourself reaching for something on the shelf only to find it has passed its use-by date?	Yes	No
• Do you frequently buy things that you think you need only to find out you already have them?	Yes	No
• Have things in your cupboard gone bad because they are not stored properly?	Yes	No
• Do you need to go to a number of different cabinets each time you bake or make a meal because you are not sure where everything is?	Yes	No
• Do you have drawers designated for utensils? Or are your utensils a jumble that you have to struggle to find?	Yes	No
• When you open a cabinet does food fall out onto you?	Yes	No

Kitchen clutter

Kitchens attract a ton of seemingly "must-have" but useless gadgets and gizmos. Tune into late night infomercials if you don't believe me! The first step to getting organized is to seriously reduce the amount of food, dishes, and appliances in your kitchen. Discard anything that has outlived its usefulness. Do you really need to keep that slow cooker just because it was a Christmas present? It's taking up valuable counter or cabinet space. And those specialty pots and pans, egg slicers, apple corers, melon ballers, and who knows what—do you *really* need and use them? One other thing—like it or not, that fondue pot needs to go!

Cabinet cleanup

Let's clean out those cupboards and drawers now. First clear off the counter so you have space to do this. Get yourself two big boxes. One is your keep box and one is your lose box. Everything you use all the time will go in your keep box. Anything you haven't used in the last six months will go in the lose box.

WORK AROUND THE "MAGIC TRIANGLE"

Think of the area formed by your sink, refrigerator, and oven or stovetop as the "magic triangle" of your kitchen. This triangle is sacred ground—the focus of food preparation, cleanup, and serving. Anything that is central to your daily food preparation (pots, wooden spoons, food storage containers, everyday dishes, etc.) should be located in or on the sides of this triangle. Nothing else should be in that area. One step out of the triangle is stuff you use regularly but infrequently: toaster oven, Cuisinart, mixer, blender, specialty pots. One step further is stuff you seldom use: bread maker, turkey pan, Christmas cookie cutters. By organizing your kitchen in this way you will find yourself moving efficiently in the space with minimum movement for maximum return. By having important and frequently used items close, you will save an enormous amount of time and energy in your kitchen.

Pots and pans

Let's start with your pots and pans. Pull everything out and stack like with like on your counter. If it will help you, write down everything you pull out. I think just seeing what you have will be enough. Are the pans in good shape? Clean? No rust? How many frying pans do you have? How many do you really need? Same with pots, baking items, mixing bowls. If you make cupcakes once or twice a year you don't need four pans, you need one. If you make stew once a year the Dutch oven that came with your pan set is enough, you don't need the cast iron oven too.

I am sure you got to the back of your cabinet and found the fondue pot, bread machine, and wedding-gift Waterford bowl that you never use but can't let go of. Put them on the counter with everything else. When all your cabinets are empty I want you to go get your camera and take a picture. All of that stuff is yours. And all of that stuff has been cluttering up the heart of your home for years. What are you going to do about it? Well, you are going to get rid of everything you don't use. Here's where those boxes come in.

Go through everything on the counter and put what you use every day in the keep box. Everything else goes into the lose box (it probably won't all fit). Now, I'll let you pull some of the lose box items out if you use them at least once a month. I bet that's not helping that much. Now, I'll let you pull out items that you use every six months—that should cover holiday baking and ice cream making. That's it. Everything else needs to go. Which box is fuller? I bet I know. Shocking isn't it? Don't worry there are a lot of people and places who will be very happy to receive what you are getting rid of. Check the Resources section for how to donate or sell the items you are letting go of.

Food

Now let's tackle the food cabinets. You are going to do the same thing with your food cabinets that you did with your pots and pans cabinets. Pull everything out and put it on your counter. Except this time, when you pull out those items check expiration dates and immediately trash anything that has expired. If you have more than one of the same item and it is still fresh and you are not about to use it to cook for 100 people put it in a pile to give to a food kitchen or pantry.

Now look at the food piled on your counter. How much of that do you use all the time? It is probably the same 80/20 ratio as your clothes. You use the same ingredients and eat pretty much the same thing 80 percent of the time. What is on the counter is all the items you bought hoping to change the way you eat and cook. Be honest. You aren't going to use them. If you find a special recipe, you'll need to buy fresh ingredients. And most likely you are not going to make something special with that jar of maraschino cherries that was on sale. Get rid of it and all that food taking up physical and psychic space in your kitchen. You should only have food in your home that is healthy and good for you and that you and your family like to eat.

Before you put back what you are keeping, wipe it all down and make sure to clean out the cabinets. Consider putting in new shelf paper—every time you open the cabinet it will be a visual reminder of your hard work and will reinforce your goal of making your vision happen.

When you put your food back into your cabinets, consider organizing it by kind and use. Store all your baking needs, canned goods, cereals together so they are easy to find. Put food your kids eat in places where they can reach them. Consider investing in clear plastic containers that will help keep your food fresh and bug free and will help you find what you are looking for. They also help you keep like things together and easily allow you to see when it's time to stock up again. To make sure you keep

CHECKLIST OF BASIC KITCHEN TOOLS AND UTENSILS

- ❏ Pots and pans (the best thing to do is to get a set of pots and pans)
    - ❏ Saucepans, two-, three-, and four-quart
    - ❏ Frying pans, eight and twelve inches
    - ❏ Dutch oven
    - ❏ Roasting pan
    - ❏ Cookie sheets
    - ❏ Cake pans
    - ❏ Muffin pan
- ❏ Steel or plastic colander
- ❏ Salad spinner (if you eat a lot of salad)

- ❑ Cutting board
- ❑ Mixing bowls
- ❑ Measuring cups and spoons
- ❑ Knives (the best thing to do is get a set of knives)
    - ❑ Chef's
    - ❑ Carving
    - ❑ Paring
    - ❑ Serrated
    - ❑ Bread
- ❑ Mixing and serving spoons
- ❑ Spatula
- ❑ Whisk
- ❑ Grater
- ❑ Corkscrew/bottle opener
- ❑ Plates and bowls
- ❑ Silverware
- ❑ Drinking glasses, cups, mugs
- ❑ Tea kettle
- ❑ Coffee maker
- ❑ Blender
- ❑ Mixer—hand or stand (if you really use it, not if you hope you'll use it.)

up on expiration dates, clip the date code from the bottom of the box and tape it onto the top of the container. Or use an indelible marker to put the expiration date or date of purchase on everything as you take it out of the shopping bag, unless you know you'll be using it within a week.

LEAST USED KITCHEN ITEMS

Take a look at the list below, are any of these culprits clogging up *your* kitchen?

Fondue pot
Breadmaking machine
Crepe maker
Ice cream machine
Vegetable juicer
Rice cooker
Crockpot
Waffle iron

Propane torch
Cookie press
Banana ripening rack
Pizza stone
Stand mixer
Anything costing $19.99 on
  late-night TV

Now, next to each item write down the last time you used it. If you used an item at least twice a year you can consider putting it on a high shelf or in the back of a cabinet so it doesn't interfere with access to the utensils that you most need on a daily basis. But before you stick them on that top shelf ask yourself: Is having this item hanging around my kitchen adding to my vision for my home? If you use any of the above less than twice a year, now is the time to remove it from your home.

Table cloths, napkins, tea towels, and aprons

Like everything in a kitchen, hand towels, table cloths, placemats, and the like have a way of multiplying. It's so easy to buy new tea towels or tablecloths but hold on to the old ones because "they still might be useful." The One In, One Out Rule stands for tea towels, tablecloths, and other kitchen/dining room linens. If you use a table cloth on your kitchen table it should be changed regularly. Make sure all the table cloths you have in your kitchen fit the size of your table. If you have holiday linens, slip a piece of paper with today's date into the fold of the linen. After every seasonal change, check your linens. If the slip of paper is still there, it's very possibly time to get rid of that item.

Of course, your needs and your cooking skills and desires will greatly influence this list. If you are a chef the items in your kitchen will be quite different from those of someone who lives on takeout. The point is that what you have in the kitchen should be the things you use the most often. It's your kitchen.

Keep like items together

Whether it is plates, pots and pans, or food items, be sure to keep similar items in the same place. Following this rule (in the freezer, refrigerator,

IN THE NIGHT KITCHEN

Because the kitchen can be so busy and there is usually a high demand for the space at certain times of day—namely breakfast and dinner time—here are some ideas on how to take the pressure off.

- Before you go to bed, get the coffee pot ready with coffee, filter, and water. All you need to do in the morning is press the on button.
- Before retiring for the night, set the kitchen table with what's needed for breakfast—plates, bowls, utensils, etc.
- Pack the kids' lunches and keep them in the fridge until they are ready to leave for school.
- Prepare some simple snacks for the kids to grab when they come home from school. That way they won't be clamoring for your attention as you are trying to get dinner ready.

cabinets, or pantry) will also save time and money as you can quickly and easily see what items you already have in stock and avoid overpurchasing.

Claim vertical space in your kitchen

Make use of the space you have. Expand the available space in your cupboards by using a lazy Susan, mini step-shelves, racks, and even back-of-door shelving systems to hold extra items. Install cup hooks to use the space under the shelves and keep your cups within reach and not stacked precariously. These are easy and inexpensive solutions that will help you avoid losing items in the back of deep cupboards.

In the spaces below, make a list of the things you will need to better use the space in your kitchen to reduce clutter and store your utensils, pots, pans, and food. By writing it down, you are making a commitment not only to acquiring these clutter corralling items but to making your kitchen fulfill its ideal purpose. Don't go crazy and buy two kitchens' worth of "space saving" devices that will only make your kitchen clutter worse. Think carefully—if your spices are all over the counter, then yes, get a spice rack to keep them contained and accessible. If the space between shelves is so great that cans are stacked one on top of the another, and you never get to the bottom, either put in a new shelf or add a mini-shelf.

Now that you know what should be in your kitchen, here's how to clean it out and truly make it the heart of your home.

THE KITCHEN CLEANSE UPKEEP

1. Keep surfaces clear and clean

A clear countertop makes any kitchen look more organized. Once the flat surfaces start to disappear under clutter, you lose your motivation to keep the area organized and you open the area to attracting more dust and dirt, further compounding the clutter problem. Consider flat surfaces your preparation area—not your storage area!

Clean as you go. More so than in any other room in the house, it's important to get into the habit in your kitchen of fully completing a task. If you are stirring a pot and splash food on the counter, wipe it up. If you are clearing the table, put the dishes in the dishwasher immediately. At the end of the meal, wash the pots and pans and rinse out the sink. This simple routine of cleaning as you go and completing a task fully will help to maintain order and cleanliness in your kitchen.

2. Keep only what you need and use

Utensils

Regular forks, knives, and spoons don't cause much trouble. But most households have at least one drawer devoted to cooking utensils—everything from wooden spoons and spatulas to garlic presses and meat thermometers. If you can, designate a drawer near the stove for utensils you use exclusively for cooking. Keep knives near your prep area.

Generally you need no more than five high quality sharp knives for food preparation. If your drawers are loaded with more than this, pare it down (pun intended). Install a magnetic strip on the wall of your kitchen

THE ONE-MONTH CARDBOARD BOX TEST

Not sure what you use and what you don't? Here is a tried and true way to find out. Empty the contents of your kitchen utensil drawers into a cardboard box. For one month only put a utensil back into the drawer if you take it out of the box to use it. At the end of the month seriously consider discarding everything that's still in the cardboard box. Face it, if it's still in the box after four weeks—you don't need it!

SHELF LIFE

Keep track of the expiration dates on bottled and canned goods. Generally these items can be safely kept, unopened, for about a year. Refrigerate after opening, being sure to transfer unused canned goods to an airtight container. Dried goods such as rice and pasta are best used within a year of purchase and should be stored in an airtight container once opened. Most spices should be discarded after twelve months as they tend to lose their flavor after that time. Store baking supplies in airtight containers in a cool, dark cupboard for up to one year.

next to the food preparation area and you'll always have quick and easy access to your knives. Get other utensils out of the drawers or other containers and sort through them to discard duplicates or damaged items. Use drawer dividers to keep them neat and accessible.

3. Regularly check food cupboards

Every six months check the contents of your cupboards and discard old food. Place all of your cooking and baking ingredients onto the kitchen countertop so that you can get an idea of how much and what you have. Put like ingredients next to each other. This regular review will mean that the kitchen clutter will not get on top of you again! When you buy new canned and boxed items, place them behind the ones that are already in the cupboard. This will guarantee that your foodstuffs are rotated and avoid having any go past their use-by date.

4. Check the 'fridge and freezer

Check and clean out your freezer every three months. Frozen foods do not keep forever—so sort through those frozen blocks at the bottom or back of your freezer. Any time you put something into your freezer label it clearly with the contents and the date. If you can't remember what an item is, chances are that it's time for it to go!

Check and clean out your fridge every week. Vegetables and fruit spoil, leftovers get pushed to the back and start to smell. Keep your fridge clean so that you can see every item you are storing. That way you won't buy something you already have and won't miss using something because you forgot it's there.

5. Keep a "magic" list

Keep a piece of paper on the refrigerator or on a bulletin board in the kitchen. This will be where you build your shopping list. When you run out of something or are close to running out, put it on the list. Let other family members know that if it is not on the list, it will not come into the house. (That's the magic!) This not only lets you keep track of what you need, it prevents needless duplication when shopping. As an added bonus it can help you organize your shopping so that you can gather coupons before heading out the door.

6. Information central

Because everyone comes through the kitchen at least once a day, it is a great place to maintain centralized information for the family. I know this is a nonfood, noneating item, but because the kitchen is in the center of the home it's a great place to keep home-base information.

- Put up a bulletin board to post notices or messages for family members.
- Post a list of contact phone numbers for emergencies and otherwise (everyone's cell numbers, office numbers, school numbers, doctors numbers, etc.).
- Put up a calendar that lists events, travel, holidays, birthdays, so everyone knows what is happening with the family and when.
- Put up mail slots or baskets for each family member so they can get their mail. Let people know if it is not retrieved in a timely

fashion it will go into the recycling bin and they may miss out on important information.

- Have hooks for keys.

DRAWER BY DRAWER

Pots and pans

Storing pots and pans is awkward and space consuming. That's why they sell those ceiling racks that allow you to hang pots attractively above your head. Another handy solution is a corner cupboard with a rotating tray that allows you to spin the contents until you find the cookware you need. Stack your pots and use an over-the-door hanger for lids or place the lids upside down on their pots to save space and stack them more easily. Go through them occasionally. See what has migrated to the back of the cupboard. Just because it's a perfectly good stockpot, if you never use it you don't have to keep it. Remember: if you have large cookware that you only use for occasional entertaining, store it high up and out of the busiest areas of your kitchen.

Food storage containers

Those plastic food storage containers seem so practical. You can never have too many, right? Wrong. Use a couple of small pieces of masking tape to seal all your containers. As you use them, you'll break the seal. After six months (preferably encompassing Thanksgiving), get rid of the containers that still have unbroken masking tape seals.

Cookbooks

Purge your recipe files and cookbooks of items that you will never use. Find an inexpensive scrapbook or file to hold all of those fantastic recipes you find in magazines or are given by friends. Keep the scrapbook with

COOKBOOK STICKY TEST

If you have too many cookbooks for your kitchen, try this simple test. Every time you use a recipe from a cookbook, mark the page with a Post-it note. At the end of twelve months, get rid of books that have no stickies.

other cookbooks in a central place in your kitchen. Discard any cookbooks you haven't opened in a year. If, by chance, you do one day need a recipe for Bavarian apple strudel custard cake there is always the Internet.

"Junk" drawer

Lots of kitchens have a "catch-all" drawer that is often referred to as the junk drawer. What's in here? It's always a surprise. It can be anything including soy sauce packets from carryout, rubber bands, pennies, matches, pushpins, or a stray refrigerator magnet. I'm only going to say this once: NO. JUNK. DRAWER. Do I make myself clear?

Plastic bags

Do you have a ton of plastic bags stuffed into a drawer under the sink? There is a push afoot to get rid of plastic bags, so you can either reuse them on your next trip or recycle them. Many grocery stores will recycle your bags, and you can recycle them yourself by using them around the house (see box). You should commit now to carrying reusable shopping bags and stop taking plastic bags. That does two things: (1) no more plastic bag clutter in your kitchen, and (2) no more plastic bag clutter in the world. Reusable bags are available now at almost every grocery store and also from sites such as ReusableBags.com. Think about carrying a com-

WHAT TO DO WITH ALL THOSE PLASTIC BAGS?

- Line small trash cans.
- Use doubled to get rid of kitty litter.
- Transport sweaty gym clothes.
- Carry wet bathing suits.
- Keep one in a bag or purse for shopping.
- Use as packing material instead of peanuts or bubble wrap.
- Use as an "umbrella protector" in your bag so other items don't get wet.
- Peel vegetables into a bag on the counter—toss when done.
- Use as shoe bags in your suitcase when you travel.
- Keep a couple in your car for disposing of accumulated debris.

pact bag that will fit in your pocket or purse so you can say "No thanks" to a plastic bag when out shopping. The environment will thank you and the clutter in your kitchen will be reduced considerably.

CREATIVE SOLUTIONS FOR KITCHEN CLUTTER

Drawer dividers. Even when you declutter all of the items that you really don't need or use in your kitchen it can be a task to keep drawers organized. You can keep like things together in your drawers more easily by installing inexpensive drawer dividers or small boxes. Simply being able to see different categories of items sitting together in your kitchen drawers will make it a pleasure to go looking for anything.

The family hub. In many households the kitchen is the central place where family members tend to leave anything and everything. Coats, school bags, mail, toys, homework, notices—you name it. Space permitting, install sturdy hooks into the wall where bags and backpacks can be hung. Label them clearly for each member of the household. You might also attach a small bag or place a labeled bin on the floor under each hook—toys, mail, or other items can be placed here for each person. This is also a great area to hang car keys and purses so that they can easily be grabbed as you leave the house.

———

Now that the kitchen is clean and clutter free, how does it feel?

_____

Make the commitment, right here and now, to keep your kitchen looking as it does at this moment.

I will commit to taking care of this room by doing the following:

Daily: Clean counter and sink, sweep the floor, empty garbage. If something is taken out, it is put away. Five-Minute Purge.

Weekly: Dust, mop, change dish towels and table cloth, clean out fridge, recycle.

Monthly: Check the use-by dates of foods in the pantry and cupboards.

Seasonally: Check what baking, decorating, and holiday supplies you used. If there were items you did not use, it's time to get rid of them.

Yearly: Stand outside the room and reassess its ideal function and if it is still achieving that function. What's getting in the way?

9

Dining Room

THE DINING AREA can be attached to the kitchen or be a separate room that is reserved for more formal occasions. I say why waste valuable space on an entire room that only gets used a couple of times a year? Use that dining room! What better place to gather with your family—at least once a week—and sit down to a meal and conversation? Who knows? You might be able to solve some of your clutter problems while you're are at it!

If you haven't done so already, take five minutes now and do a quick surface clean so you can more easily get down to the nitty-gritty as you work over this room and return it to its ideal function. Look back at your vision board and your initial answers.

THINK IT THROUGH

Few surfaces in the home are greater magnets for clutter than the dining room or kitchen tables. That beautiful large flat surface practically cries out for things to be left on it—wrapping paper, bills, the mail, yesterday's homework, and piles of "I'll get to it later" clutter.

This is another room that the family shares, so it's good to get their feedback too.

Stand in the doorway/entrance way to your dining room. Write down your responses to the following questions:

• How do I feel when I enter the dining room?

_____

• How do I *want* to feel when I enter this room?

_____

• What is this room's function now?

_____

• What is the function I want it to have?

_____

• In order to serve its function, what furniture, contents, and open space should the room contain?

Furniture: _____

Contents: _____

Open space: _____

- Take a look at your dining table. How does it look right now?

_____

- How would you like to use the table?

_____

- Does each item in this room enhance and advance the vision I have for the life I want?

_____

- How do we imagine using the space?

Self: _____

Spouse/Partner: _____

Child: _____

Child: _____

Child: _____

- What is the consensus on how this space is to be used?

_____

- What is getting in the way of this space being used in the way we imagine?

_____

• What needs to be done or changed to use the space in that way?

_____

The dining room table should be considered sacred space in your home. It is a TV-free gathering place where the family has regular opportunity to talk about issues affecting them and to reiterate their visions for the life they want to live as individuals and as a family. I'm not saying you should sit down at the table and say, "Let's reiterate our visions," but when we talk to each other about what happened that day, or how we want to spend the weekend, or what is annoying us, we're creating that vision.

SET IT UP

Now, let's take a minute and pull together all the hard work and thought you have put into envisioning your ideal dining room. Write it down here as a touchstone for the work you are about to do to get this room in shape.

Goals (from page 33): _____

Ideal function (from page 47): _____

What has to go (from page 56): _____

_____

What it should contain (from page 58) _____

MAKE IT HAPPEN

As you clean out the dining room, take the time to clean behind the hutch and other furniture, check to see that all chair joints are tight and the upholstery is intact. Take a look at the curtains, blinds, or drapes and see if they need attention—at the very least, give them a good cleaning. Think about the last time you painted the room. Are you still satisfied with the result?

MAPPING YOUR ZONES

The purpose of the dining room is to have a pleasant place in which to enjoy time with the family while you share a meal. A clean, uncluttered dining area helps maintain calm and relaxation when you gather together. Remember: This is your dining zone—everything that doesn't contribute to that function should be removed. Keep it simple and elegant.

The zones in your dining room are:

- Eating.
- Storage space for dishes.
- Formal china.
- Entertaining supplies.

Eating

The dining room table can end up the focus of family activity. Everything from crossword puzzles and model airplane building to homework and gift-wrapping can happen here. Make it a rule to clear the area when each project is finished so that the table is always available to everyone and ready for mealtimes. No cheating. The table is always kept empty. Consider keeping the dining table covered with a tablecloth so it appears ready for its primary use.

When you look at the table, think about how you dine or entertain.

- Is there space enough for your entire family?

- What needs to change to accommodate the whole family?

  _____

- Does the table fit the room?

  _____

- Is the furniture you have suited to the space you have made for it?

  _____

- Is there adequate lighting?

  _____

- Could you have a meal at this table at a moment's notice?

  _____

- If not, why not?

  _____

Storage space

Walk into your dining room and imagine you are explaining to someone how you most use this room.

- Does what you see match with how you use it?

  _____

- How do you use your dining room and what types of meals do you have there?

  _____

  _____

- Do you need and use all of the flatware and glasses that you currently own?

  _____

- How many people use these items?

  _____

- How often do you entertain?

  _____

- Are they usually small, intimate gatherings or large family affairs?

  _____

With your answers in mind, take out all of the plates and dishes that you use for meals and arrange them on your dining room table.

1. Gather matching flatware and glasses together on the table.
2. Discard any that you no longer like or use as well as any that are chipped or damaged.
3. As you return these items to your cupboard or hutch, place what you use most frequently within easiest reach. Large serving platters

and anything that you use infrequently should be placed on the lowest or highest shelves or at the back of the cupboard.

Formal china

If you have formal china, do you guard it as if it were a national treasure? China can be expensive and beautiful, but what's the point of owning it if you never use it? Please try to enjoy it. But please don't keep family china if it isn't meaningful to you. If you really must save it in case your children like it more than you do, put it someplace where accessibility isn't a factor. And if no one really likes it, then off to eBay or a consignment shop or Craigslist you go!

Don't hold onto china just because you think it is valuable or may be valuable "one day." The time and effort you spend storing it or moving it from home to home and never using it isn't time or money well spent. Find out if it is worth something right now. If not, give it way, donate it, or sell it.

Formal glassware

Water goblets, brandy snifters, old fashioned glasses, highball glasses, red wine, white wine, and champagne flutes are just some of the types of glasses you may have purchased or received as gifts (particularly wedding gifts). Glasses are often left on the shelf out of fear of breakage or damage. I say, if you are scared to use the glasses, it's probably a good idea to sell them off or otherwise get rid of them. Why should they take up space in your hutch or cabinet that could house things that you will use and enjoy?

Linens and napkins

Take out all of your linens and napkins and group together those that match. Look them all over carefully and decide what will stay and what will go.

1. Discard anything that is stained or torn beyond repair.
2. Discard anything you haven't used in the last year.
3. Discard anything that you wouldn't be proud to have on your table.
4. Discard anything that doesn't fit your current table shape or size.

If possible, it's a great idea to keep all of your table linens, tablecloths, and napkins in your dining room. Some people prefer to hang large tablecloths in a closet—if that works best for you by all means do so.

Assign a drawer or shelf for linen sets so that anyone setting the table or putting things away can easily see where things belong. Keep the "informal" tablecloths together and separate from the more formal tablecloths. If you are short on space, visit your local hardware store and purchase a shallow drawer that can be attached to the underside of the dining room table. Keep linens clean, dust free, and readily accessible. But don't keep them around if they are stained, torn, or otherwise unusable. Toss what you don't use so you will have room for what works for you.

Serving pieces and utensils

If you have silver serving pieces and utensils you may find yourself only using them on special occasions. This if fine, but if those occasions are few and far between you might want to rethink why you are holding onto them in the first place. It's like your jewelry—it can sit in a drawer or you

PROTECT YOUR INVESTMENT

To protect good china and flatware invest in cloth storage sets that provide special protection for special-occasion china and stemware. These protectors zip closed and come with foam-padded dividers and foam separators for placement between each plate to avoid chipping and damage.

can use it and enjoy it. I say get it out in the light of day and if it doesn't enhance the vision you have of your dining table, your home, or your life then let it go! Your silver should be stored in such a way that it is protected from tarnish—either in a special box or in cloth bags that reduce the chances of tarnish marring your prized items.

Other entertaining supplies that you will want to keep in your dining room or dining area are candlesticks and candles, serving plates, and serving utensils.

Once you have got your dining room sorted out, you can set the tone as to how formal or informal you would like it to be. Dining rooms can be a place for a special meal or entertaining but who says pizza night can't get a bump up and be in the dining room every once in a while?

Doesn't it feel great to have a space where you can entertain family and friends over a meal free of clutter?

———

Now that the dining room is clean and clutter free, how does it feel?

_____

Make the commitment, right here and now, to keep it looking as it does at this moment. I will commit to taking care of this room by doing the following:

Daily: Keep the table clear. If something is taken out, it is put away. Five-Minute Purge.

Weekly: Dust, vacuum, wash soiled linens and napkins.

Monthly: Be sure glassware, plates, and utensils are clean, damage free, and stored properly. Polish silver. Assess if the clutter is still out of the room.

Seasonally: Check your linens. If you haven't used something this season, it's time to get rid of it.

Yearly: Stand outside the room and reassess its ideal function. Is it still achieving that function? What's getting in the way?

10

Bathroom

BATHROOM PRODUCTS ARE INEXPENSIVE and tempting. They smell so good! They make promises about changing your skin, your hair, your life. But it's very important to keep bathrooms clutter free. Mold, mildew, germs, and grime love clutter—especially in a warm damp space like a bathroom. It's close to impossible to keep it clean and hygienic if there's stuff everywhere. Remember your vision board—even if you didn't create a vision for your bathroom, refer to your original questions to remind yourself of your goals for the house and for this space.

THINK IT THROUGH

It's easy to accumulate products, but to keep your bathroom clean and clear you are going to have to weed out the little-used products and keep only what you use, love, and enjoy.

Write down your responses to the following questions:

- How do I feel when I enter this room?

_____

- How do I *want* to feel when I enter this room?

_____

- What is this room's function now?

_____

- What is the function I want it to have?

_____

- In order to serve its function, what furniture, contents, and open space should the room contain?

Furniture: _____

Contents: _____

Open space: _____

- Does each item in this room enhance and advance the vision I have for the life I want?

_____

SET IT UP

Now, let's take a minute and pull together all the hard work and thought you have put into envisioning your ideal bathroom. Write it down here as a touchstone for the work you are about to do to get this room in shape.

Goal (from page 33): _____

Ideal function (from page 47): _____

What has to go (from page 56): _____

_____

What it should contain (from page 58) _____

MAKE IT HAPPEN

You will be pulling items out from under the sink and from the medicine cabinet. Use this opportunity to clean the shelves, replace any storage bins that are broken, get a new shower curtain, and consider a splash or two of paint to spruce up the room.

MAPPING THE ZONES

The bathroom comprises two primary zones—the personal and the products.

Personal zones are the spaces designated for each person who uses the bathroom on a regular basis. Give each family member his or her own storage area and bathroom caddy, which can be kept either in a bathroom cupboard or in the bedroom.

Sink

This area should be kept clear. I'll allow soap, toothbrushes and toothpaste, and a drinking glass. All else should be in individual caddies or put away in drawers, a cabinet, or on shelves. Clutter around the sink can lead to damage from becoming damp, or to mold, mildew, and other unsightly and unsanitary conditions.

Solving sink clutter

1. Rinse toothbrushes out and put them in a place where they can dry completely between uses.
2. Teach everyone to put the cap back on the toothpaste when done!
3. Rinse the sink when done with brushing and flossing.
4. Replace toothbrushes every six months and after any major illness (to prevent reinfection).
5. If space is tight teach everyone to take their caddy with them when they are done in the bathroom.
6. Be sure there is a wastebasket.
7. Regularly discard out-of-date or unused cosmetics and medications.

Tub and shower

Only the items that are currently in use should be found in the tub or shower. Don't let the old soap turn to a gelatinous mass under the new soap. Does every family member using this bathroom need to have his or her own shampoo, conditioner, and body wash? Come on, be real. It's just soap. And even soap can be clutter.

Transforming the tub and shower

1. Clear out any unused or finished potions, lotions, soaps, including old body wash (anything over six months should go), old razors, etc. Toss or recycle the containers.

COSMETIC CLEAN UP

All makeup has an expiration or use-by date. Sometimes it is stamped on the product itself, sometimes on the packaging. Regardless, most makeup goes bad in six months! A good rule of thumb, however, is that the closer the product is used to the eyes, the shorter the lifespan.

- Mascara—four months.
- Eye creams and face creams—six months or so.
- Liquid cosmetics, such as foundations—one year.
- Lipsticks and pencils—one to two years.
- Eyeliner—indefinitely (if in pencil form and sharpened before use).
- Powdered products, such as eye shadow, blush, and face powder—up to three or more years.
- Perfume—three years. (Some perfumes have a manufacture's code on the bottle, for example, AJ6543. The last number, in this case 3, indicates the year in which the perfume was made.)

It is always better to keep cosmetics away from moisture and humidity, so if you keep them in the bathroom, be sure to have them in a drawer or other container.

2. Remove the bath toys that are no longer used. Plastic bath toys are a prime target for mold growth.
3. Have a place to hang washcloths so they can air properly. (If you don't have a rack in the shower, you can use suction hooks or hangers.)

4. Check loofahs, puffs, bath sponges, and scrubbers for mold, mildew, and bacteria. Wash or discard as needed.
5. Check your shower curtain for mold or soap scum. Replace as needed.
6. Have a hair guard on your drain and discard any hair captured after each shower.
7. Rinse the tub/shower daily.
8. Clean it weekly to prevent mold, mildew, soap scum buildup.

Medicine cabinet

All prescription medications, vitamins, and anything toxic should be kept in a safe place away from children. This includes over-the-counter family medicines like flu and cold treatments and digestible first aid supplies. Other items like Band-Aids should be in a common area.

Managing the medicine cabinet

1. Open the cabinet.
2. Item by item, shelf by shelf, check the expiration date of the over-the-counter drugs (and vitamins) in the cabinet. If a staple has passed its date or you have run out (e.g., children's medications, ibuprofen, Band-Aids, etc.), be sure to add to your shopping list.
3. Clean out any prescription medications that you no longer need. Check any ongoing prescriptions that need to be refilled. If you are disposing of prescription medications, check the prescription information for proper disposal. To avoid the risk of medications being ingested by someone who shouldn't have them, take drugs to your local pharmacy for proper disposal.
4. Check batteries in your thermometer.
5. The print on many medicine containers is very small. Consider keeping a pair of magnifying glasses in the medicine cabinet for those late nights when you are bleary eyed and need to get the dosage right.

6. Put a small box on the shelf for items like nail clippers or tweezers. It will be easier to find them that way.

Closet, cupboard, and under the sink

Keep extra supplies like soap, shaving cream, or toothpaste in an area away from the most heavily trafficked spots in the bathroom. This will help you to see quickly what you have and avoid unnecessary purchases. It will also help you know when it's time to replace something. Keep some cleaning products in a plastic caddy under the sink so that you have quick access to the sponges, sprays, and wipes you need to keep the room spotless.

If you buy in bulk, keep a few backups in the bathroom and store other items in your pantry or closet outside of the bathroom.

Consider replacing any harsh chemical-based cleaners with organic or environmentally friendly cleansers. They usually smell better and are easier on the environment—in your home and the world at large.

Unearthing what's under the sink

1. Take everything out of the cabinet or cupboard.
2. Examine each item and see if it is still usable (the empty sunscreen container, anything that has expired, bits of paper, products that are no longer used by the family—for example diaper rash cream for the baby who's now in first grade).
3. Toss out what you can no longer use.
4. Consider grouping like items in baskets (sunscreens, personal hygiene products) so they can be found easily.
5. Put most-used items (supply of toilet paper rolls) at the front of the shelf; lesser used items (hot water bottle) toward the back.

USE VERTICAL SPACE

If you have trouble keeping flat surfaces clear in the bathroom, look to the available vertical space you have. Install hooks or towel rods on the back of the bathroom door or use over-the-door hangers for towels and robes. Install a hook to hang your blow dryer.

If there isn't enough shelf space for the towels that are not in use, consider rolling up your towels and storing them in a basket on the floor.

Install shelves or cabinets that allow you to neatly store many of the items that live in the bathroom. Maximize your vertical space by purchasing an over-the-toilet cabinet. Baskets, small containers or trays are a great way to keep like things together. Put medications in one, hair products in another, first aid materials in a third, and so on.

Shower caddies now come in many shapes and sizes. Some hang from the showerhead or are attached to a tension pole that fits into the corner of the shower. Invest in one that is sturdy, easy to clean, and large enough to hold the different shower products used by members of your family.

Your bathroom is now clean and clutter free. Don't you feel more refreshed when you use it yourself?

———

Now that the bathroom is clean and clutter free, how does it feel?

_____

Make the commitment, right here and now to keep it looking as it does at this moment.

I will commit to taking care of this room by doing the following:

Daily: Put cap back on toothpaste, rinse sink, rinse shower/tub, clear drain of hair, hang up towels, Five-Minute Purge.

Weekly: Empty wastepaper basket, clean mirrors, tub, toilet, towels in laundry.

Monthly: Assess what products haven't been used. Replace anything that's needed. Assess if the clutter is still out of the room.

Yearly: Stand outside the room and reassess its ideal function. Is it still achieving that function? What's getting in the way?

11

Garage, Basement, and Other Storerooms

GARAGES ARE STUFF CEMETERIES. Just because you have the space doesn't mean you have to fill it. In fact, the thing that should fill your garage first is the car—that's what it's there for. Beyond that a garage (and basements, attics, and other storerooms) can be legitimately used for genuine storage. But *only* if the items deserve the space and are stored in such a way that you can easily access what you need when you need it.

THINK IT THROUGH

Garages and storage areas can be tough places to declutter and get organized because everything with no place in the house usually gets shoved in there. It can be the black hole of storage. Well, it's time to get some light in there!

WATCH WHERE YOU PUT THAT!

Beware of the downside of certain spaces when it comes to storing your possessions.

Garage—If unheated, can be subject to climate extremes. Can be damp.

Basement—Can be damp. Will be the first place to flood. Not a great spot for important papers.

Attic—Heat rises, so can be warm. Roof can be an access point for squirrels and other rodents.

If you have limited storage space, use it as best you can and store items in such a way that they will be protected from the adverse conditions they are stored in. After all, if you are storing something, it's important and should be protected, right?

The garage and basement, unless they're finished rooms, are usually used by the adults in the family. Make sure you include everyone who uses these rooms in the cleanup strategy. Stand outside your garage or storage area. Write down your responses to the following questions:

• How do I feel when I enter this space?

_____

• How do I *want* to feel when I enter this space?

_____

- What is this space's function now?

_____

- What is the function I want it to have?

_____

- In order to serve its function, what should it contain?

Furniture: _____

Contents: _____

Open space: _____

- Does each item in the space enhance and advance the vision I have for the life I want?

_____

SET IT UP

Now, let's take a minute and pull together all the hard work and thought you have put into envisioning your ideal garage or storage area. Write it down here as a touchstone for the work you are about to do to get this space in shape.

Goal (from page 34): _____

Ideal function (from page 47): _____

What has to go (from page 56): _____

_____

What it should contain (from page 58) _____

MAKE IT HAPPEN

Before you begin, take a minute to prioritize what you want in your garage (or other storage space). List below, in order of importance, what you want to keep here. Hint: if you are working on your garage, the car must be number one!

1. _____

2. _____

3. _____

4. _____

5. _____

6. _____

Once you have prioritized and made your list, you have a better sense of how to approach the cleanup. If you are hesitant to let something go, let your list be your guide.

Start slow

Let's assume we're working on your garage—although everything here equally applies to any storage area in your home. It has taken months or even years for your garage to become cluttered so it may not be realistic to try to organize everything in one day or even a weekend. If this is the case for you, commit to starting small—one section of the garage at a time. Make a commitment every day to declutter and organize another section until it's done.

Streamline

Get rid of items you haven't used in over a year. If you haven't touched something in twelve months, chances are you are never going to use it. Do all those seasonal decorations actually get used? What about that sports equipment? Forget the excuses. Now is the time to free up space by letting go of unused and unneeded items.

Return what you've borrowed!

If there are any tools or items that aren't yours, return them to their rightful owner. If you are storing things for a friend, neighbor, or family member and the stuff has overstayed its welcome—make a call and get them to come pick up their things. It's a good idea to label tools with a permanent marker so that if you do lend them out they will find their way back to you.

Get stuff off the floor

Once items start spreading across the floor it's almost impossible to keep them under control. Use vertical space to increase your storage capability and to avoid "floor creep"! Install a good, sturdy shelving system to store the items you decide to keep. Remember, though, that you only have the space you have. The volume of stuff, the number of boxes, or the size of storage containers is determined by the shelving space you have. Don't overload the garage just because you have the space!

Invest in hooks or other items specifically designed for hanging and organizing tools.

Jump in at the deep end!

If you are a brave soul, once a year drag everything out of your garage. Get the whole family involved. Commit to getting rid of 50 percent of what is stashed in the garage. Take the car out of the garage and go through all boxes, bins, and storage cupboards. Be brutal! If you aren't using an item—get rid of it.

Look up

Consider using the ceiling of your garage for storage. Most hardware stores carry a wide variety of hooks that can be used to hang bikes, sporting gear, or even gardening tools. Items like storm windows or summer window screens can easily be stored on ceiling rafters. Ladders can go up there too. Remember: you are creating useful storage, not space to hide away clutter you've removed from the rest of your house. All it takes is a little creativity to discover new storage solutions to old problems.

Maintaining the space

Be sure you have a sturdy push broom to reduce the amount of dust and dirt in your space. Whenever you wash your car, take the time to sweep out the garage. At the end of the day, return tools to their proper places. If you have a clear space for something, it shouldn't take more than a minute to put it back.

MAPPING YOUR ZONES

Establishing clear zones for various items and functions is critical to your garage or any storage space. Storage size and issues may vary but the general zones needed are below. Consider color coding different areas.

You can install an orange pegboard for tools, paint the wall green where the kids hang their bikes, use blue hooks and bins for sporting gear. Be sure to clearly label any box, bin, or container that goes into the garage so that items can be easily and quickly located. Consider different colored labels for boxes or containers of like things. This will help everyone in the house see where things belong and encourage order from the chaos. Maintaining zones in your garage will also help avoid unnecessary purchases and assist in keeping things organized and tidy.

Garage zones include:

- Gardening/lawn supplies.
- Laundry.
- Workbench.
- Tools.
- Paint and chemicals.
- Sporting gear.
- Seasonal items.

Gardening/lawn supplies

Keep a basket (hanging from a hook) for often used gardening tools—trowel, hand rake, gloves, hat. You won't waste time searching for them when you are ready to garden and you'll have more time to spend in your flowerbeds. Lawn maintenance supplies should be kept together as well. That way you can get what you need whenever you need it.

Getting a grip on gardening stuff

1. Designate an area in the garage for gardening materials.
2. Gather gardening materials from where they may be around the garage. Be sure to collect watering cans, the wheelbarrow, rakes, etc., and put them all in one spot.
3. Add hooks for things like hoses (which should be coiled and hung for winter) and sprinklers.

4. Smaller items like trowels and grass clippers can be kept in a bin (clearly labeled) to keep them from damp and rust. They should be wiped down after each use.
5. Taller items like rakes, garden stakes, or ladders can be hung or leaned on the wall.
6. If you have duplicate items, get rid of them.
7. If you have bags of chemicals, fertilizer, or peat consider putting them in storage canisters to keep out damp as well as pets or children.

Laundry

A laundry area should have some shelves where you keep detergent, fabric softener, and bleach; a table or space where you can fold laundry; and a hanging rack for anything that doesn't go in the dryer.

Laying out the laundry area
1. Give a thorough cleaning to the top and inside of the washer and dryer. If you are cleaning your clothes in these machines they should be clean as well.
2. Be sure the lint trap is emptied each time you do a load in the dryer.
3. Check detergent, fabric softener, etc. to be sure you have enough and that tops are tightly closed.

Workbench and tools

Like any horizontal surface in your home, the top of the workbench is prone to becoming covered with stuff that doesn't belong. Keep the surface clean and either use a peg board or bins for various tools and equipment. Coil and hang extension cords, keep nails, bolts, and screws in small containers, label shelves so everyone knows where things should be returned to when done.

Making the tools and workbench work

1. Collect all of your tools and lay them out on the workbench.
2. Determine if you have any duplicates and decide which *one* of something you will keep. (Varying sizes of tools are fine—you just don't need two hammers of similar size and weight.)
3. Get rid of (sell or give away) any tools you got for a special project that is now completed or tools that are never used.
4. Sort nails, screws, and bolts, and store them in small clearly labeled containers (clear containers are great for this). If you don't have clear containers or are using small drawers, affix a sample of the nail on the outside of the drawer that has that kind of nail in it. Do the same for screws, bolts, nuts, etc.
5. Keep a toolbox with essential items—hammer, flathead screwdriver, Phillips-head screwdriver, assorted screws and nails, pliers, and measuring tape. That way, when you have things to do in the house you can easily carry your tools with you.
6. Set up a pegboard at the workbench and once you have determined where the tools will go, draw an outline of the tool with permanent marker so there is never any question of what goes where.

Paint and chemicals

Paint and chemicals should be stored securely and out of the reach of children and pets. Paint cans seem to accumulate in garages or basements because we hold onto them for future use or touchups. Consider putting the paint into a smaller container when you have completed a large job. It will be less likely to dry out, and become less of a storage issue as well.

Putting paint in its place

1. If you have paint left over after a project, tape the color chip to the top of the can before you store it. That way you'll know immediately what's in the can and can get new paint if you need it.

FYI—GARAGE AND BASEMENT SAFETY

Do not store highly inflammable items like kerosene, paint thinner, or gasoline in your basement or garage unless they are in tightly sealed containers in a closed—and preferably locked—cupboard. Ensure that your basement and garage, like the rest of your home, are fitted with smoke detectors and keep a fire extinguisher handy. Keep a clear clutter-free space of at least eighteen inches around your furnace to avoid a potential fire hazard.

2. Check old paint cans to see that the paint is still usable.
3. Get rid of any paints that no longer match the rooms in your home.
4. Check with your local government to find the best way to get rid of paints or other chemicals in a safe and environmentally friendly way.
5. Next time you buy paint look for environmentally friendly paint—rest assured, it comes in colors other than green!
6. Be sure brushes and rollers have a place to hang or be stored where they can dry out completely once they have been cleaned. Discard rollers if they do not clean throughly. You can't paint well with a stiff roller.

Sporting gear

Sporting gear can be anything from bikes to baseball gloves. When multiple members of the family engage in multiple sports you have the potential for sporting gear overload. Again, keeping like things together is the key.

Sorting your sports stuff

1. Bins, a coat rack, pegboard, or cupboard can keep sporting gear sorted and ready to go when needed. Use a plastic barrel for long items like baseball bats, lacrosse sticks, and skis.

2. A bin for each family member is a great way to keep on top of who uses what equipment.

3. Be sure any sports bags are opened, emptied, and aired out after they have been used. You don't want to find a sweaty hockey sock that's been fermenting in a bag for months (or even days or weeks!).

4. At the end of a sports season, take an inventory of the wear and tear on your equipment (and assess the fit for children's gear). Discard what is worn out or too small and replace as needed.

5. Donate or hand down items the kids have outgrown. Chances are there is another season's use in them.

Seasonal decorations and wrapping paper

The neat thing about seasonal items (from a professional organizer's perspective anyway) is that every time you take them out or put them back away you have an opportunity to assess whether you really need to keep them. If you didn't use that glow-in-the-dark skeleton this Halloween, ask yourself if it's really worth storing away for another year. More than most things stored in a garage or basement, it's the seasonal decorations that often are a cause of tension. If you have the space and they're stored properly, that's great. If not—you know the drill!

Wrapping paper

I should admit upfront that I am not a big fan of wrapping paper—well, at least not what most people think of when they use the term. Personalizing gifts by using distinctive wrapping paper isn't necessarily a bad thing, but if your home is overrun with wrapping paper it may well be time to do something about it.

There is a simple and elegant way to manage the wrapping of gifts. Remember the principle: More is not necessarily better! Purchase a roll of good quality brown paper and high quality ribbons of three colors— black, red and white. Wrap all your gifts in this simple brown paper and decorate with any selection of the ribbons. Is brown paper too dull for you? Use the same approach selecting your "signature" color. This minimal approach will mean that your gifts will always stand out and that you will not have to spend a fortune on wrapping paper. Best of all, these supplies take up negligible room. Elegance in simplicity—it really does work!

LUGGAGE

If you travel, you will need a suitcase or bag to bring your clothes with you. It's easy to think you need different sizes and different bags for different trips—the carry-on, the overnighter, the weekender, and so on. Before you know it you have five suitcases when all you really need is one. And these bags are probably multiplied with every family member. Not to mention the backpacks, sling bags, sports bags, messenger bags, briefcases that everyone needs on a daily basis. It's enough to make your house look like a storage locker! Time to clean out that locker. Check over all of your bags and luggage. Are they worn, do the zippers work, does the pull-out handle function properly, are the wheels running smoothly? If something is broken, get it fixed. If it is unusable, toss it out. Is there something from your last trip still packed in there? Luggage is one of those things that gets held onto because you "might need it someday." Store it efficiently so you can get to when you do need it. Consolidate by putting smaller bags inside a larger bag. That way you only have to look in one place when you suddenly need a carry-on for a last minute trip.

THOSE MYSTERY BOXES

You may have boxes that are still unpacked from your last move. You may have boxes of wedding presents or gifts you received and because you didn't know what to do with them you parked them in the garage—probably instead of the car! Well, I think by now you know what I am going to say.

1. Determine what is in each and every box in your garage, basement, and/or storage area.
2. Take the items out of the box and decide if they fit your vision of your ideal home and life.
3. If not, they need to go.
4. If they are important to you, then you need to ask yourself why they are sitting in a box in the garage rather than being honored and enjoyed by you and your family. If you value an item and want to keep it around, it must have a place to live where it will enhance your life and not cause clutter.
5. Seasonal items or clothes you are holding onto for the kids to grow into should be stored in clearly labeled bins, boxes, or containers so you know what you have and can get to it when you need it. I'm a big fan of clear storage boxes and bins because there is no mystery as to what's inside.

Things you'll need to declutter and reorganize your space.
Often when a space is decluttered the need to purchase items to organize what you're keeping disappears. You may well find that the bins or containers you already own are more than adequate to meet your storage and organization needs. If not, there are some basic items that may help:

- Storage bins/containers of various sizes (hint: keep like items in the same size and style of container—it will be easier to find what you need).

- Labels.
- Toolbox.
- Shelving.
- Pegboard.
- Push broom and dust pan or hand-held vacuum.
- Waste can.

Because the garage can be a dumping ground for a wide range of items, it can also be a challenge to get clean and clear. But now that it is sorted, you have a place to keep your car and still have room for tools, sports equipment, and more. Your garage is living up to its purpose as functional storage for things you value, use, and enjoy!

―――――

Now that the garage is clean and clutter free, how does it feel?

_____

Make the commitment, right here and now to keep it looking as it does at this moment.

I will commit to taking care of this room by doing the following:

Daily: If something is taken out, put it away. Do a Five-Minute Purge.
Weekly: Empty waste basket, sweep, be sure lint trap on dryer is clean.
Monthly: Assess what is or isn't being used in the garage. Assess if the clutter is still out of the room.
Yearly: Stand outside the room and reassess its ideal function. Is it still achieving that function. What's getting in the way?

12

Sanctuary

I BELIEVE THAT EVERYONE'S HOME, no matter what the size or location, should be a haven for all who live there. A home is where you laugh, love, learn, play, eat, relax, grow, entertain, and more. No matter how large or small, a home should be about the quality of live you want, not the quantity of stuff you can acquire. Because of the importance of the home to the health and well-being of every family member, I believe it is essential to clear away the stuff and start living. That's what this book is all about: Clearing space so you can live your life. As you know by now, it's not about the stuff.

Together we are creating the ideal vision for your life and your home and making it happen. It is about clearing out the clutter so you have a clear pathway to health, happiness, and relationships with your family members.

Family is wonderful but we all need a space in the house where we can unwind, be undisturbed, and pursue a hobby or interest without interruption. These spaces are sanctuaries—an oasis of calm away from the hustle and bustle of the world. Don't underestimate the power of peace and quiet. Now that your home is sorted out and you and the family are maintaining a clutter-free lifestyle, it is time to claim some space for yourself.

• Where do you find calm in your home?

_____

• Is the only option to go into the bathroom and lock the door?

_____

• Ideally what would be in a space that would allow you to feel as if you were in a sanctuary?

_____

• Where in your home can you imagine making that space?

_____

• Go to that room or area of your home. What is there now?

_____

• What would have to change to make it your solo space?

_____

• What will you have to do to make it separate from other zones or areas in the room?

_____

- If you are lucky enough to have a whole room at your disposal, what needs to be done to make it a calm, inviting space?

  _____

- Can you share the space with other family members? Can you make a sanctuary space in your home that everyone can use?

  _____

- Remember when you did vision boards of your home and the rooms in it? Time to do the same thing for your sanctuary space.

  _____

- If your home is constantly full of family, friends, and neighbors, and space is at a premium, is there a time of day when you can give yourself the gift of solitude? Claiming something for yourself, whether physical space or a quiet few minutes on the back porch with a cup of decaf, is a wonderful gift to yourself.

  _____

- What about your spouse and kids? They need to rest and recharge too.

  _____

- Can a corner of a kid's room become his or her sanctuary?

  _____

- What would it need to be made into that space?

  _____

- Is there a space your child goes to now to unwind or escape from the fray?

  _____

- Does your spouse retreat to the den, basement, or workroom after returning home from work?

  _____

- Where do you first go when you come home?

  _____

My sanctuary will be: _____

The things I need to make it my space are: _____

_____

_____

_____

I will need to communicate the following to my spouse/partner and kids

about my sanctuary: _____

_____

Part II

Keeping It Clutter-Free

13

Maintenance

THINK BACK TO THE VISION you had for your home when you started this workbook. Has it changed as you have done the work in each room of the house? Take a minute now to think about your home. In the space below write down what your vision is for your home, right now.

_____

_____

_____

_____

Now, write down a few key words (cozy, welcoming, fancy, hi-tech) that express your ideal for each room in your home:

Master bedroom _____

Kid's bedroom _____

Family room/living Room _____

Home office _____

Kitchen _____

Dining room _____

Garage/storage _____

Other _____

These character traits of the rooms in your home will serve as your guideline on what you will allow in each room going forward. Anything that doesn't fit your vision for a space in your home doesn't belong there. To keep you on the straight and narrow, there are three immutable rules for keeping clutter out of your home.

The golden rules:
- Every room has a purpose.
- Every thing has its place.
- Your home reflects who you are.

It's not just spring cleaning

This process of decluttering isn't something you trot out once a year or do out of desperation when company is coming. It's a lifestyle change that allows you to make the most of the space you live in and make it truly your own. To keep your home functioning at its best (and a clean home can keep you at yours as well) you need to follow some guidelines.

DAILY

If you get it out—put it away.
If you open it—close it.

If you finish it—replace it.

If it's full—empty it.

If you take it off—hang it up.

If it's dirty—wash it.

If it's garbage—trash it.

Every day schedule five minutes for the Five-Minute Purge.

The Five-Minute Purge

1. Set a time each day (morning or evening or midafternoon—it's your choice). When you commit to a time each day, it will become a habit.

2. Pick your target. Make sure to keep it small so you can be thorough. Choose one drawer in the kitchen, one shelf of video tapes, the floor of the coat closet, etc.

3. Grab a medium-sized garbage bag. You'll use this bag to throw things away or to drop them off at your charity of choice, whichever makes more sense for the items you're purging.

4. Set the kitchen timer for five minutes.

5. Clear out anything you haven't used for the last six months to a year. You were supposed to have done this when you first cleaned your home, but a home is a living thing and what you felt you needed to keep yesterday, you may be able to let go of today. Be ruthless. The more you get rid of, the longer you can wait before you revisit this area.

6. When the timer goes off, stop. If the bag is full, put it in the garbage (or in your car trunk so you can drop it off the next time you drive past a Goodwill or other charity). If the bag isn't full, put it with the garbage or recycling in preparation for tomorrow, when you'll surely fill it up in your next purge.

Are you carrying your clutter with you?

Purse purge

Do you have back pain from lugging around a purse that's too big and too full?

1. At the end of each day, empty your purse and sort through it, with the same eye you would use in going through your closets or drawers.
2. Toss receipts, bits of paper, wrappers, tissues, etc.
3. Consolidate where you can—bring makeup essentials, not your makeup drawer.
4. Carry a small brush or comb not a salon-sized one.
5. Don't carry all of your credit cards around with you. Notwithstanding the inconvenience of losing them, fewer credit cards in hand mean fewer purchases to clutter your home.
6. As you take each item out of your purse, ask yourself, "Why do I have this in here?"
7. If the answer is "It's for just in case or I might need it" then it's going to have to go.
8. Only carry with you what you need on a daily basis.
9. Lighten your load and you'll walk with a lighter step.

ORGANIZING YOUR CREDIT CARDS

All credit cards have emergency contact numbers on their reverse side—however, this is not much use if you lose the card or if it is stolen. Place all of your credit cards on a photocopying machine and makes copies of the front and rear of the cards. Place the copies in a safe place. If your cards are lost or stolen you have a complete record of their numbers.

The car cleanse

If you spend a lot of time in your car, an enormous amount of clutter can build up in a short amount of time. But if you make the commitment to a daily car cleanse you will be happier riding around town.

1. Toss out empty beverage containers.
2. Keep a small plastic bag in the car to collect refuse from eating on the road and dump it at the end of the day.
3. Refold those maps and put them in the glove compartment.
4. Get anything out of the car that doesn't belong. Don't use your car as additional storage. Don't leave the sleeping bag from your last camping trip in the back seat of the car because you have "no where else to put it." It doesn't belong in the car.
5. Open the trunk and clear out anything that doesn't belong. The things that should be here are spare tire, tire iron, jack, or other emergency items. This is not the place for the bags from your last shopping trip (that you are hiding from your spouse/partner).
6. Each month clean and vacuum the interior and wash the exterior. If you live in areas with snow and they use salt on the roads it is a good idea to rinse the undercarriage of the car in the winter months to remove the corrosive salt.
7. Be sure to schedule regular maintenance checkups—oil change, winterizing, etc.

WEEKLY

Conduct a zone check once a week. Depending on the size of your home you can do one room or more each week but be sure you maintain a rotation so no room gets left out of the process.

For the room you are checking you will be making sure that there hasn't been any zone creep (dad's crafting materials have migrated to the place where mom pays the bills) or any misuse of zones (Junior's ice hockey equipment is in the family room) or any zone bloat (the DVDs no longer fit in their allotted space on the DVD shelf).

If you police your zones weekly, a clutter situation will not get so out of hand that you will become overwhelmed and unable to cope.

If you do laundry each week, see it as an opportunity to discard or give away clothing that is worn out, doesn't fit, or is otherwise no longer needed.

MONTHLY

Once a month have everyone do a Five-Minute Purge of his or her own room. Younger children can be helped through the identifying and ridding the room of the things that don't belong. Common rooms can be done at this time too. Get as many family members in on the act as possible. The more people, the quicker it gets done. And if they have been made responsible for returning items to their proper places it is more likely they will take ownership for keeping the room(s) neat and organized.

SEASONAL

Conduct a seasonal switch (see pages 89–90) for your room, the kids' rooms, and the hall closet (for coats, jackets, etc.). Don't forget about the yard or patio. Bring in furniture, garden hoses, and the like.

Winter—Break out the hats, gloves, scarves—check wear and fit.
Spring—Transition from cold weather clothes to lighter wear.
Summer—Get bathing suits out and check wear and fit. Designate a beach bag and keep towels, sunscreen, etc. loaded in it so you are ready to go.
Fall—Back to school and prep for the holidays.

YEARLY

Review and revise your vision. Are you living up the vision you originally had for your home? Have your circumstances changed (a new baby, elderly parents moved in, Junior off to college) so that you need to revise the way you see your home? Reevaluate how your home reflects who you are now and act accordingly.

A RULE AND TOOLS FOR KEEPING A LID ON CLUTTER

The One In, One Out Rule

Remember when you taught your kids about getting rid of an old toy to make way for the new? Well, this rule applies to everything in your home. One pair of new shoes in, one pair out. It's more challenging if you are upgrading, like to a new TV, and the old TV works fine. It may be tempting to put the old TV in the kitchen or a bedroom. Before you do, ask yourself if the TV fits the vision you have for that room. If not, it shouldn't go in there.

It's OK to revise your vision, just be sure it is a conscious choice, not one made out of necessity or convenience.

The charity bag

A charity bag can be kept in a bedroom or closet. Essentially, it is where you will put things that have never been worn or are gently worn that you no longer need. You can decide where they go from here—a local charity, Goodwill, The Salvation Army, a friend or neighbor—but they do need to go. Remember to be respectful of the recipient of these items and be sure they are clean and neatly folded. (See Resources for information on donating used clothing and other items.)

Cleaning equipment

You can't get control of clutter and keep things clean without the right equipment.

- Vacuum.
- Broom and dustpan.
- Mop and bucket.
- Dust cloth.
- Sponges.
- Cleaning products (like in the bathroom, treat yourself and your home to low-chemical organic products).

Be sure to designate a spot for cleaning items and make sure it is easy to get to. The easier it is to clean the more likely it is that it will get done.

Job chart

You can't make use of the cleaning equipment unless you have a plan. And one that can involve the whole family.

Name	Monday	Tuesday	Wednesday	Thursday	Friday	Saturday	Sunday
Dad	Empty dishwasher 10 minutes						

Have everyone keep track of the household chores they accomplish in a single week and the time they spent on each one.

At the end of the week, compare results. Using the above exercise, redistribute chores to even out the time each person spends cleaning up and helping out. Create a job chart. Your job chart can include tasks like:

- Sorting mail.
- Doing laundry (kid friendly).
- Folding laundry (kid friendly).
- Taking out trash (kid friendly).
- Paying bills.
- Setting the table (kid friendly).
- Doing the dishes (kid friendly).
- Straightening your bedroom (kid friendly).
- Walking the dog (older kid friendly).
- Feeding pets (kid friendly).
- Cleaning up after pets (kid friendly).

A REMINDER ABOUT THE COST OF SPACE

No matter whether you own or rent your space, you're paying per square foot. I'm not going to make you do the real math here, but when you lose your ability to enjoy a room or to store your expensive car in a proper garage, you're throwing that portion of your rent or mortgage out the window. When you move to a bigger home (or just fantasize about it) because you can't throw things away, you're throwing good money after bad.

When you rent storage space you're wasting money, not solving the problem. Now what's so bad about renting storage space, you ask? It's a way of not dealing with your clutter. You're saving things you don't need or want by dumping them in a black hole you'll probably never unpack, and you're spending extra money every month to store them.

Think about it from a financial standpoint. You're increasing your housing costs without increasing your standard of living. Is it worth it? Think about it from a psychological perspective. You're hiding away stuff you really should deal with, postponing the issue to some undetermined future date. Is that how you deal with all of your problems? I sure hope not. Look, if you have a sudden change of situation, okay. I'll cut you some slack. But as soon as you've rented the space for longer than a year, you have to accept that your situation isn't temporary. Your life has actually changed. You need to deal with the change head on.

Do you have things in storage? How long have they been there?

_____

What is in the storage space?

_____

Where is it?

_____

Why is it there?

_____

How much are you paying for that storage space? Yearly?

_____

When was the last time you were at the storage facility?

_____

If, for some reason, the items in storage were lost to you forever, would they be missed?

FYI—SELF STORAGE MANIA

The first self storage facilities appeared in Texas in the late 1960s. Today approximately 10 percent of American households have items in one of the 40,000 self storage facilities in this country. This is a 75 percent increase from just ten years ago and has happened during a time when the size of the average American house has increased by half. Larger houses *and* more stuff in storage!

14

Cleanup Checkup

DECLUTTERING AND GETTING ORGANIZED takes commitment, focus, and, initially, a significant time commitment. By now you should see some major changes in your home, your sense of well-being, and your attitude toward the things you have decided to keep. You know if you're winning the battle—you see the clear surfaces, feel the open space, have new, efficient routines, and experience the sense that anything is possible.

HOUSEHOLD SUMMIT

Now it's time to meet with your family and discuss what you did and didn't achieve.

Are you able to use each room in your house for its intended purpose?

_____

Did compromises solve the clutter and cleaning problems?

_____

Is your partner happy with your shared living space?

_____

Are your kids more relaxed and focused?

_____

Are you proud of your space?

_____

Is the anxiety about clutter gone?

_____

Is there a harmonious relationship between your home and the life you want to live in it?

_____

Ask your children specific questions about whether their reorganized spaces work for them.

Is it easier to find your toys?

_____

Do you have enough space to do your homework?

_____

Do you enjoy working at your arts table?

_____

Do you put your things away when you're finished with them?

_____

How is watching DVDs in the family room instead of mom and dad's room?

_____

Do you like eating in the dining room with the whole family?

_____

Is there anything else that would make your space more enjoyable for you?

_____

_____

Ask your partner bigger questions about life.

Do you feel relaxed now when you get into bed?

_____

Do you feel there is a sense of balance and calm in our home?

_____

Do you feel clear about what we both hope to gain from the lives we are living?

_____

Is there anything you think you could change at home to bring it closer to the life you both imagine?

_____

_____

_____

If your home is still feeling a bit out of control, it's time for a bit of remedial work. Here's a little exercise I like to call the Trash Bag Tango, and it goes something like this: First, stop buying everything but the essentials, then grab two trash bags. Every day for a week take ten minutes to go around your home and fill one bag with trash—old papers, torn and unusable clothing, out of date magazines—anything at all that you'd classify as garbage. Fill the other with items that you want out of your house. (Remember? The "out the door" items.) Maybe you want to give them to a friend or family member or even to a charity. If you want to sell items in a yard sale, or online, grab a third bag and fill it with those items. Just a consistent ten minutes a day is all this technique asks of you. Commit to this and you will see some significant changes.

Do this every day for a week and you'll notice a huge difference.

Do it every day for a month and everyone else will notice a huge difference.

Do it every day for three months and you'll conquer the clutter in your home.

Once you've got basic clutter conquered, you need to set up a plan and system to keep the clutter at bay. A house is a dynamic system that needs to adjust to accommodate changes in the family, the things they value, and the things they possess.

15

New Rituals

WHO WANTS TO SACRIFICE a whole Saturday to cleaning up the mess that your house has become? Who wants to spend the day before you host a party straightening up when you should be prepping food or getting a manicure?

The secret to staying organized and maintaining a clutter-free home is to make organization a natural part of your life. Regularly clearing the clutter is great but it may not be enough to cope with the changes that can happen in any household. Things fall into disrepair. New hobbies fall by the wayside. You outgrow clothes. Stuff accumulates. The holidays arrive. Even the best intentions can get sidetracked, and your weekly bag-in-hand clutter control may have slipped a bit. The best way to manage the never-ending clutter creep is to establish an annual cycle of organization.

BEYOND SPRING CLEANING

We all know that spring has traditionally been a time of cleaning—after a long winter the home was aired and every corner was scrubbed clean. This ritual dates back to old English times. Well, times have changed. Before the industrial age people had less and homes were smaller. Clutter was not an epidemic. Spring cleaning is still a great tradition, but it's time for a new, year-round set of traditions that will help keep your home organized and clutter free.

A YEAR IN THE LIFE OF AN ORGANIZED HOME

JANUARY—START FRESH

1. Purge the holiday decorations
- → Discard old, unused, or broken decorations.
- → Limit decorations to the space you have.
- → Clearly label the boxes in which they are stored.
- → Use different boxes for each holiday to avoid confusion and help keep order.

2. Use the right storage containers
- → Divided boxes for tree ornaments.
- → Flat, sectioned boxes for wreaths.
- → Large plastic stackable bins are great for lights, decoration, and larger seasonal items.
- → Label containers clearly and store them in the less trafficked parts of your home or garage.
- → Consider numbering bins and creating a master list of what each contains.

3. Holiday in/out
- → Examine your haul and see what items of equivalent size and use can go.
- → Pack up what needs to go and get it to someone who can use it. (See Resources.)

FEBRUARY—SHRED MANIA

1. Get a jump on your tax return
- → Prepare your taxes and file as early as you can to ensure a quick refund.
- → Discard and shred financial records and other documentation that you no longer need to back up your returns.
- → Label and file current tax records.
- → Go through important papers, files, and documents and throw out or shred old files or paperwork that you no longer need or use.
- → Update any insurance policies or legal documents such as wills as appropriate.
- → Make a photocopy of any new policies, credit cards, or other critical documents acquired in the last twelve months and store the copies away from your home in a secure location.

2. Create a message center
- → Designate a specific area in your home to post announcements or invitations, a family calendar, and messages.
- → Hang your keys and keep your loose change in this area.
- → Mail should be processed right nearby. Have a paper recycling bin/basket handy.
- → Post (and update) frequently used numbers and emergency contacts.
- → Divide the board into areas for each family member so that everyone knows where to post a note or message for someone specific.

MARCH—REINVENT SPRING CLEANING

Create a task list for your family. Revise as needed for your particular situation.

Spring Cleaning Task List	Person Responsible	Materials Needed
INSIDE		
Clean windows.	_____	_____
Dust and clean tops of cabinets and electric appliances.	_____	_____
Steam-clean carpets.	_____	_____
Launder winter bedding and blankets before storing.	_____	_____
KITCHEN		
Deep clean all appliances inside and out.	_____	_____
Thoroughly clean inside cupboards and refrigerator.	_____	_____
Discard outdated food items from your pantry and freezer.	_____	_____
Organize like items together around the magic triangle.	_____	_____
Discard pots, pans, and utensils that are seldom or never used.	_____	_____
Clear all flat surfaces.	_____	_____
Restock kitchen cleaning caddy.	_____	_____
Thoroughly clean the black hole under the sink!	_____	_____

CLOTHES

Discard clothes that you no longer love, wear, or look great in. Donate unwanted items to your favorite charity.

_____ _____

Arrange like items together in your closet.

_____ _____

Sort your clothing by color so that you can clearly and easily see what is in your wardrobe.

_____ _____

Store away winter clothes.

Replenish cedar blocks or moth balls to protect from moths and insects.

_____ _____

OUTSIDE

Remove storm windows, make sure they're labeled, and then store carefully to avoid damage.

_____ _____

Clean outside of windows.

Store your snow removal equipment.

_____ _____

Do a quick maintenance check on your lawnmower and other gardening equipment. Reseed and fertilize your lawn.

_____ _____

Check your garden hoses and breathe the first scents of spring.

_____ _____

APRIL—EXPLORE THE BLACK HOLE

1. Divide and conquer
→ Divide your home into four areas and tackle any storage closets in one zone each week during this month. The four areas might be basement, bedrooms, living areas, and laundry—choose areas that make sense to you.

→ Start with the Five-Minute Purge or Trash Bag Tango. Get down to serious clutter removal by sorting items into what you'll keep, trash/recycle, or give away/sell.

2. Spread the load
→ Ask friends or family to help if the amount of stuff in storage is large.

→ Volunteer to return the favor.

MAY—DISCOVER THE GREAT OUTDOORS

1. Prepare for the great outdoors
→ Check and fix outdoor play equipment: swings, slides, bikes, etc.

→ Fire up the grill to make sure it's in working order.

→ Hose off outdoor furniture and (if you're lucky enough to have one) make sure your pool equipment is in working order for those long hot days ahead.

→ Bikes, in line skates, and other sporting equipment should be tuned up for use or tossed out if they are not being used.

2. Plan a summer vacation
→ Now's the time to use all that money you made in yard sales or saved by not buying things you don't need.

→ Gather the whole family together to talk about summer possibilities and plans.

→ Involve everyone in the planning and decision making.

→ Divide tasks so that everyone has a role to play in organizing the family vacation.

3. Organize kids' summer activities
→ Work with your kids to schedule their summer vacation activities.
→ Mark camp dates, trips to the pool, beach, or museums on your calendar.

JUNE—TEACH YOUR CHILDREN WELL

1. Tackle your kids' spaces
→ Make a project of their personal space. What's working? What's not?
→ Identify as many zones as make sense for your child—reading, clothes, homework, crafts, computer games, laundry.
→ Work with your child to make sure that items are in their correct area.

2. Make the closet kid-friendly
→ Make sure your child's closet suits him or her.
→ Are her favorite things easily accessible?
→ Make room by putting off-season items high up on shelves, get everything but shoes off the floor.
→ Buy or build appropriate storage containers for the things she needs every day.
→ Help your child decide which clothes and shoes it's time to discard.

3. Tackle the toys
→ Gather old toys, games, and books that are no longer used or age appropriate.
→ Consider establishing a give-away bin or a broken/lost toy bin so your child can make these decisions part of regular cleanup.

→ When you go to make the charity dropoff, bring your children along so they can make the donation themselves and learn the value of giving to others.

3. Limits and routines

→ Reinforce those agreed upon limits.
→ Make it part of your household routine to identify items that need to be donated to charity or sold in a yard sale.
→ Without the pressure of school, create or revise a schedule of chores.
→ Make sure you and your child agree that the chores list will still work when school starts again and homework becomes a factor.

4. Rewards

→ Make the projects as fun as you can.
→ Find a balance between organization and play.
→ Spread projects out throughout the summer.
→ You might go to the pool every Saturday after addressing one of the zones in your child's room.
→ Keep everything on a calendar which you and your child discuss and anticipate.

JULY—HAVE A YARD SALE

1. Go online and make a dollar

→ Consider using an online auction site.
→ Sporting goods, electronics, brand-name clothes, jewelry, collectibles, and automotive parts are some of the items that generally return great prices online.

2. The yard sale

→ For all those items you don't want to sell online, organize a yard sale.

TRADING ASSISTANTS

There are companies that will sell your stuff on eBay for you. They're called trading assistants and can be found at the eBay site. If you're not tech-savvy or you never seem to find the time to sell things on eBay, it's worth paying the commission to let these folks handle your goods. They take your stuff (gone!), photograph it, sell it online for you, ship it, and send you a check less their commission. No more hoarding boxes and packing materials in anticipation of an eBay selling spree that never happens. No matter how little it turns out your stuff is worth, it's all found money.

YARD SALE PLANNING:

Set a date. Do this well in advance, **at least six weeks** prior. Don't choose a holiday weekend. Pray for good weather.

Tell your neighbors. **At least four weeks before**, let your neighbors know about the sale—encourage them to have a sale on the same day. The more sellers, the more people you'll attract to the sale.

Permits. Many communities now require a permit. It would be good to find out about that well in advance.

Decide what to sell. **Two weeks** before the yard sale, supply everyone in your family with a box or two that they can fill with items that they want to sell.

Collect sale items. **One week** before, gather boxes and all other items into the garage.

Tell the world. **At least one week before.** Yard sales are all about advertising. Put large colorful signs on all major roads. Keep all signs the same color with clear directions, the address, and the time. Use humor to draw the crowds. Take out ads in the local paper and put notices in local supermarkets or other places that have community notice boards. Try listing the yard sale online or in free community newspapers also. Email friends and family and ask them to do the same.

Attach price tags. **One week before**, clearly price everything with masking tape and bright markers. Put like things together. Use tables to make the viewing of merchandise easier. Borrow clothing racks. Have a great layout of goods so that people can easily see everything.

Enlist helpers. **Two days before**, assign your helpers specific tasks like managing the crowd, answering questions, making sales, taking payments, and keeping you laughing. Make sure everyone knows what they are responsible for and how to do it.

Be prepared. **One day before**, have an extension cord handy so people can check electric items. Have shopping bags or boxes handy to help people collect and carry goods away.

Get some sleep. On **the night before** the sale put a sign in front of your house that reads: "Absolutely no early birds" or else you'll have people knocking at your door before the sun is up.

Check your signage. On the **day of** make sure all signs are still in place and legible.

Manage the money. On the **day of**, have a lot of small change handy—use a fanny pack to keep the money safe and in one place.

Bargain. On the **day of** the yard sale, the idea is to get rid of everything. Bargain like crazy—offer to add items for an extra fifty cents. Five books for the price of three, four shirts for the price of two—you get the idea. **An hour** before you are due to finish, slash prices to clear the merchandise!

Get rid of everything. **After the sale is over**, arrange for a charity to pick up whatever is not sold. Bag it and put it in the car if you need to take it yourself.

Don't take anything back into the house! (Except your profits from the sale.)

AUGUST—PREPARE FOR BACK-TO-SCHOOL

1. Clothes and gear
- → Check your child's school clothing to make sure they have not outgrown it.
- → Make sure your child has a sensible backpack and wet weather gear.
- → For younger kids, purchase and hang a five-pocket clothing bag so that a week of clothes can be laid out in advance of the school week.

2. Home office and school supplies
- → Stock the home office.
- → Check your children's school supplies.
- → Organize the items so they are easy to locate and replenish items where necessary.

3. Shopping for school
→ Ask your children to draw up a list of what they think they need for the new school year.
→ Check together against what they already have.
→ Use the resulting list as a basis for planning a shopping day.
→ Consider giving them a budget and letting them make some purchases.

4. Digital cleanup
→ Set aside a few hours on a slow night to declutter and organize your computer files and digital assets.
→ Delete old files; archive important files that are no longer active, delete poor quality photos, post favorite photos to online sharing sites or save them to CDs and send out to family and friends.
→ Download and install a desktop search tool like MSN Search's "Windows Desktop Search" to help you easily find items anywhere on your PC, including emails and attachments, in the same way a search engines searches the web for you.

SEPTEMBER—MAKE THE SEASONAL SWITCH

1. Make space in your closets
→ Use a closet in the guest bedroom or another suitable space in the basement or attic to store your off-season clothes.
→ Make sure the storage location is cool and dry and that all stored clothes are clean.
→ Moth balls or cedar blocks will help keep moths and other pests at bay.

2. Discard what you no longer wear
→ Every time you switch clothes for the season you should give your closet a quick once-over.

→ Get rid of things you haven't worn as well as damaged or soiled clothing.

OCTOBER—BRACE YOURSELF FOR WINTER

1. Garage cleanup

→ Take everything out of the garage, sweep out dust and debris and hose down the floor. Discard unused items, arrange like items together, and install sturdy shelving to clear items off the floor.
→ Park the car in the garage where it belongs.
→ Install shelving, a peg board, and racks for sporting goods, tools, and storage bins.
→ Establish zones and label everything clearly.
→ You can even mark areas on the floor for the kids' bikes.
→ If the garage is a tight fit for your car, install mirrors to make parking easier.

2. Winterize the house

→ Clear gutters of leaves and debris.
→ Have your chimney, fireplace, and furnace inspected.
→ Make sure all your gardening tools and equipment are properly stored out of the weather. Install storm shutters.
→ Check doors and windows for drafts and reseal accordingly.

NOVEMBER—GEAR UP FOR THE HOLIDAYS

1. Entertaining

→ Prepare for any meals and events you may be hosting using a planner like this to get you started.

Done	Task	Person Responsible	Materials Needed	Rented	Borrowed or Purchased?	Prep Day
	Create a final guest list					
SERVING DISHES						
	Cups					
	Plates					
	Utensils					
	Serving platters					
	Serving utensils					
	Napkins					
	Pitchers					
	Punch Bowls					
FOOD						
	Chips & dip					
	Brownies					
	Crudités					
	Pigs in a blanket					
	Nuts & candy					
	Cheese & crackers					
	Ham					
	Garnishes					
BEVERAGES						
	Ice					
	Beer					

	Wine				
	Soda				
PARTY FAVORS					
DECORATIONS					
	Balloons				
	Candles				

2. Holiday card and gift lists
→ Consider using a PDA or a computer to electronically store names and addresses so that you can quickly and easily print name and address labels for your holiday cards.
→ Use it to save the addresses from the envelopes of cards you receive.

3. Take notes
→ Keep a list with the gift idea, the person it's for, and the date you had the idea on a page at the back of your daily planner. When it comes time to shop the list will jog your memory.
→ If it's been several months you might want to check with someone in the know to make sure your recipient hasn't already bought or received the item.

4. Consider giving an "experience" rather than a "thing"
→ A concert or theater ticket, restaurant gift certificate, or even a donation to a particular charity can leave a more lasting impression than another gadget or unnecessary article of clothing.

5. Keep the gift giving under control

→ It's nice to be generous, but don't go overboard. Gifts can account for a large chunk of clutter because they tend to be items with value that aren't exactly what you want or need.

→ Suggest that the family or group set a price limit on gifts, use a family lottery to choose one person only to buy for, or only purchase gifts for the kids.

PULL THE REINS IN ON HOLIDAY GIVING

- If you have a large family, at Christmas draw names out of a hat. Next year, you're responsible for giving to the person you pick.
- If you have a large family, consider only giving gifts to the kids.
- Give disposable gifts or gifts that don't take up room (gift certificates, food baskets, charity donations, etc.) to business associates.
- Before you even start shopping, decide on a number of gifts that you're buying for your kids. Stop when you're done.
- Get your child one and only one big ticket item like a bicycle or a dollhouse.
- Immediately donate to charity gifts that are age-inappropriate or duplicates of things your child already owns.
- Do a pre-holiday purge.

When you give, be sensitive to the clutter issues your friends and family may have. Make it a policy to always give a gift receipt. That way it can be exchanged.

6. Go digital and save some legwork
→ Shop online—it's easy, fast, and shipping is often free around the holidays.
→ If you're traveling, have gifts shipped directly to your destination.
→ Save yourself a shopping trip, and spare yourself those impulse purchases that tend to go hand-in-hand with holiday shopping.

DECEMBER—RELAX AND ENJOY

1. Don't beat yourself up
→ Enjoy the season, enjoy your family, and enjoy yourself! Be happy about your successes, be clear about where you feel you failed, and be realistic about what you can achieve in the New Year.

2. Celebrate your successes
→ We seldom make time to reflect on our dreams or our achievements. Set aside time to think how you've tried to live a simpler, richer life with less junk.

3. Commit to making the changes you want
→ The number one New Year's resolution in America is to lose weight. For the coming year why not consider shedding the extra weight of clutter that fills your home and bogs down your life.
→ Commit to removing two garbage bags of items a day from your home—one of trash and one of items you're donating to charity—until the clutter is under control.

———

There's no way around it: clutter doesn't clear itself. Staying ahead of it takes time and effort. I'm not a magician. But I can promise you that if you create new traditions, the clutter will never get out of control and the words "It's all too much!" will never cross your lips again.

16

Control the Inflow

ONCE YOU HAVE GOTTEN a handle on clutter in your home and established new rituals for your daily, weekly, monthly, and yearly cleaning and organizing you will be in great shape. However, as I've mentioned before, while it is important to keep things flowing out of the house, you have to keep a close watch on the things that are coming in. The primary culprits for overcrowding are indiscriminate spending, impulse buying, and "retail therapy" that allow us to acquire without evaluating what we are buying, why we are buying it, and where it is going to go once we get it home.

There is nothing wrong or bad about purchases like video games, DVDs, or books—some of them are educational or entertaining—but how many of them have lasting value? What do you have to show at the end of any one year for the money you have spent? Is it a home equipped with valuable and useful items or just more clutter?

Don't forget that the money that you spend on stuff you never really use could have been saved for something life changing—a vacation, or a child's college tuition. Is the stuff that costs money and fills up your house what makes you happiest, or would you be happier with less stuff and access to that long-gone money? And, if you are paying by credit card and don't pay the bill in full each month, it's possible that you will be paying for an item long after you brought it home and then decided that you didn't like it or it didn't fit where you thought it would.

WANT VERSUS NEED

Separating what you want from what you need will go a long way toward reducing the flow of stuff into your home. Before you shop, take the time to think about what it is you are looking for and why you are buying it. Needs have to do with sustenance, shelter, and health. Wants can run the gamut from the necessities to the ridiculous. Whenever you find yourself about to put something in your shopping cart (actual or virtual) ask yourself, "Is this something that I need, or that I want?" Other essential questions include:

Where will it go? Is there room?

What will I remove to make room for it?

Is there another way (e.g., rent, borrow) I can enjoy this without purchasing?

Is it on my shopping list?

Essential shopping tips
- Before you shop for clothes, review what is in your closet. Because you have organized it by style and color (right?) you can easily see what you need.
- Make your list and carry it with you in your wallet or purse.

- Don't just write down "pants." Be specific about the type or style, e.g., black wool pants. Don't forget size, especially if you are buying for another family member. If you find yourself grabbing other clothes, remind yourself, "What am I here for?" and use your list as your guide.
- If you veer from your list, decide (before you buy) what is going to have to go in order for this new item to come into your closet and into your life. It's the old One In, One Out Rule in action!
- Remember, a bargain isn't a bargain if you get it home and can't use it or don't wear it. Don't be seduced by the super marked down discount sale price. If you wouldn't buy it at the full price on the ticket or it isn't on your list, don't buy it at all.
- A list is especially helpful during the holidays. It is easy to get caught up in the frenzy of the season and find yourself with too many items that you don't need.
- For big ticket items like TVs, refrigerators, or furniture you need to make a couple of assessments before heading off to shop.
  - First, determine what you will do with the old one when the new one comes in.
  - Next, measure your space and write down what will fit in the area you have.
  - Then, determine your budget. If you write down a price range you are less likely to be persuaded to get something beyond your means.

With smaller items you should ask yourself if there is another way to enjoy the items without bringing any additional materials into the house. Can a book be borrowed from the library? For DVDs, can you subscribe to a service like Netflix, rent it, or borrow it from the library so that you can view a movie without having to create shelf space for it? Can you organize a game trade with friends or neighbors so that you can swap games rather than each purchasing a new one?

Impose a forty-eight-hour time delay on all purchases over $25.00. If you cannot purchase something unless you have let forty-eight hours pass then you'll give yourself time to consider whether you really need that item or not.

If you plan to shop at a particular store for a particular item, bring only that store's credit card with you. If you are shopping in a mall, you won't by tempted by the other stores around you.

Establish an experience fund. Every time you stop yourself from making a spontaneous purchase put the money that you would have spent in a special account called your "experience fund." Pick something that your whole household can look forward to—a trip to Paris, the beach, Disneyland, for example. If your child asks for a toy at the store, you can do the same thing. Say, "This toy costs $9.99. Let's put that in the Disneyland fund instead." At the end of twelve months I promise you'll have enough money to have an experience that the whole household will remember forever.

RENEW, REUSE, RECYCLE

There are many ways that you can lessen your impact on the planet, while at the same time reducing your outgoing costs. There is an old saying, "Use it up, or wear it out. Make do, or do without." These can be watch words for keeping rampant spending in check but can also help to keep a handle on your environmental impact. Not only is it important to recycle cans, bottles, paper, and plastic, but you can engage in a little green living in your own home.

- Rather than automatically heading off to the mall when something has a small stain or is slightly damaged, see if you can repair or refurbish it. New upholstery or slip covers on a couch or chair can give a new life to furniture that has become a little tired.
- Try repurposing what you already have. Can the small rug you don't want in the den anymore be used in a larger room to demarcate space for the kids' corner?

- Reheel or resole shoes that have become worn or broken but still have many miles on them.
- Consider shopping at consignment or thrift shops. You can get great bargains and you will not be adding to the impact manufacturing goods have on the earth.
- Search online for groups like Freecycle, FreeSharing, or Sharing Is Giving (organizations that connect people who have things they want to throw away with others who can use those things—see Resources section) to find a new home for your old couch rather than throwing it out and having it end up in a landfill.
- Pass hand-me-down clothes to a friend or neighbor. The clothes will get a second life and you can help to ease their budget.
- Ask your local library or school if they are in need of books, DVDs, or games and pass them on when you, or your child, are finished with them.

When we clean clutter out of our own homes, *some* of that clutter may be functional or useful to someone else. The items themselves aren't inherently clutter because, as I've said before, it's not about the stuff. Someone else may need that item to help complete the ideal function of their home. By the same token, always be respectful of the people or organizations you are passing your things onto.

————

Wow! We are here at the end of another wonderful journey together. I hope that the exercises in this workbook have helped you to forge a new path that leads you to a clutter free life in surroundings that bring you joy.

Take some time to celebrate your new approach to living—have a friend come over right now and show off your spotless kitchen. Email your college roommate and brag about your sanctuary. Thank your family for all the hard work they have done and will continue to do.

Enjoy your home and your new way of living in it!

Appendix

ROOM FUNCTION CHART	
MASTER BEDROOM	
Current function	
Ideal function	
Who uses it?	
Who should use it?	
What should it contain?	
What has to go?	
KID'S ROOM	
Current function	
Ideal function	

Who uses it?	
Who should use it?	
What should it contain?	
What has to go?	
FAMILY/LIVING ROOM	
Current function	
Ideal function	
Who uses it?	
Who should use it?	
What should it contain?	
What has to go?	
HOME OFFICE	
Current function	
Ideal function	
Who uses it?	
Who should use it?	
What should it contain?	
What has to go?	

KITCHEN	
Current function	
Ideal function	
Who uses it?	
Who should use it?	
What should it contain?	
What has to go?	

DINING ROOM	
Current function	
Ideal function	
Who uses it?	
Who should use it?	
What should it contain?	
What has to go?	

BATHROOM	
Current function	
Ideal function	
Who uses it?	
Who should use it?	

What should it contain?	
What has to go?	
GARAGE	
Current function	
Ideal function	
Who uses it?	
Who should use it?	
What should it contain?	
What has to go?	
ROOM: _____	
Current function	
Ideal function	
Who uses it?	
Who should use it?	
What should it contain?	
What has to go?	

Resources

Charity Navigator
An independent charity evaluator. A great source for finding a charity to suit your needs.
charitynavigator.org

Dress for Success
The mission of Dress for Success is to promote the economic independence of disadvantaged women by providing professional attire, a network of support, and the career development tools to help women thrive in work and in life.
dressforsuccess.org

The Cinderella Project
Provides prom gowns and accessories for girls in need.
Check for chapters in local areas via your web browser.

Goodwill
Collects toys, clothes, furniture, etc. and sells them in their stores to raise money which is used to help people in need find jobs.
goodwill.org

Salvation Army

Family Stores provide quality clothing, furniture, and other goods to the community at bargain prices. 100% of the proceeds go directly to the operation of The Salvation Army Adult Rehabilitation Centers.
salvationarmyusa.org

National Furniture Bank Association

Provides families in need with used furniture.
help1up.org

World Computer Exchange

World Computer Exchange is a global education and environment nonprofit that helps connect youth in 65 developing countries to the skills, opportunities, and understanding of the Internet while keeping working computers out of landfills.
worldcomputerexchange.org

Computers 4 kids

Collects and refurbishes computers for low income youth.
c4k.org

Computers for Schools

Computer for Schools offers certified refurbished computers to schools and nonprofits at about 1/3 of the cost of new.
pcsforschools.org

National Cristina Foundation

Not-for-profit foundation dedicated to the support of training through donated technology. For more than two decades they have encouraged companies and individuals to donate computers and other technology, which is then matched to charities, schools, and public agencies in all 50 states, Canada, and in many countries around the world.
cristina.org

The Global Literary Project, Inc.

Donates books and literacy support materials as well as conducting educational programs.

glpinc.org

Darien Book Aid

Sends books in response to *specific requests* from Peace Corps volunteers, libraries, and schools all over the world. Books are also donated to libraries, prisons, hospitals, Native American, and Appalachian groups in the United States.

dba.darien.org

The International Book Project

Serves long-term emerging literacy needs around the globe and at home, as well as responds to areas impacted by natural and humanitarian crises. Their mission is to promote education and literacy while broadening Americans' understanding of their neighbors.

intlbookproject.org

Swap Tree

Free exchange/trade of books, DVDs, videos, and CDs.

swaptree.com

Freecycle

The Freecycle Network™ is made up of 4,643 groups with 6,199,000 members across the globe. It's a grassroots and entirely nonprofit movement of people who are giving (and getting) stuff for free in their own towns. It's all about reuse and keeping good stuff out of landfills.

freecycle.org

FreeSharing

The sites featured on FreeSharing.org are all locally owned, grassroots groups, working to help their neighbors and the environment by keeping usable items out of the landfill by passing them along to people who can use them.

freesharing.org

Sharing Is Giving

Sharing Is Giving is a "link only site" to direct potential members to recycling sites.

sharingisgiving.org

Free Use

Offer or seek a reusable item—furniture, clothes, appliances, computers, toys, a pile of dirt, plants, books, used moving boxes—and all things in between.

freeuse.org

Toy Swap

Swap, buy, or sell new or gently used toys.

toyswap.com

Network for Good

A website where you can give to your favorite charity/charities and have all your donation records stored and accessible at any time.

networkgood.org

File Solutions

Filing system materials and information.

filesolutions.com

Freedom Filer

Filing system materials and information.

freedomfiler.com/Home.cfm

Quicken

Personal finance software.

quicken.intuit.com/

Norton AntiVirus

Program for screening out computer viruses.

symantec.com

Spybot Search and Destroy

Program for protection from spyware.

safer-networking.org

Direct Marketing Association

Reduces the amount of direct mail—credit offers, catalogs, magazine offers
you receive.

dmachoice.org

Opt Out

Run by the consumer credit reporting companies (Equifax, Experian, Inno-
vis, and TransUnion it will remove your name from preapproved or pre-
screened offers of credit or insurance.

OptOutPrescreen.com

888.567.8688 (888.5OPT.OUT)

41 Pounds

Paid mailer removal service. $41.00 for 5 years.

41pounds.org

Reusable bags

Bags, water bottles, and more.

reusablebags.com

EBay
On-line auction site.
ebay.com

Craigslist
Classifieds.
craigslist.com

About the Author

Described by *The New York Times* as "a genius," Peter Walsh is a noted international organization expert, bestselling author, TV personality, and radio host who characterizes himself as part-contractor and part-therapist.

Peter is the author of the bestselling *How to Organize Just About Everything* and *It's All Too Much: An Easy Plan for Living a Richer Life with Less Stuff*—upon which this workbook is based—which has been translated into many foreign languages and appeared on nine bestseller lists including both *The New York Times* and *The Wall Street Journal*. His book exploring the relationship between clutter and weight, *Does This Clutter Make My Butt Look Fat?: An Easy Plan for Losing Weight and Living More* was released in February 2008 and also quickly became a *New York Times* bestseller. Peter's exploration of mental clutter, *Enough Already!: Clearing Mental Clutter to Become the Best You*, was released in March 2009.

Peter is currently a regular on *The Oprah Winfrey Show* where he coaches viewers to "declutter their homes, their heads, their hearts, and their hips so that they can live better lives." He also hosts a weekly national radio program as part of the Oprah Radio network that can be heard on XM156 and Sirius 195. During the last four years, Peter also starred as the tough-love professional organizer in more than 100 episodes of the TLC hit show *Clean Sweep*.

As well as being an expert in organizational design, Peter is also an experienced educator and a skilled motivational speaker. Born and raised in Australia, he moved to Los Angeles in 1994 to launch a corporation to help organizations improve employees' job satisfaction and effectiveness. His company, Peter Walsh Design, has helped thousands of home owners and corporations organize their living and work spaces for optimal efficiency and liberated living.

Peter now lives (clutter-free) in Los Angeles and travels extensively, both nationally and internationally, working with private clients, shooting organizational programs, and for public speaking and consultation engagements.

Further details about Peter and his company Peter Walsh Design, Inc. may be found at peterwalshdesign.com.